# SELLING TO WIN

# ◀ ABOUT THE AUTHOR ▶

Richard Denny is one of the UK's foremost authorities on sales
and management training – a distinction that has earned him a
place in *Debrett's Distinguished People of Today*.

He is Chairman of his own highly successful company Results
Training, a major management training company, and the writer
and presenter of the video course *Profession Selling* – a world
bestseller.

Thousands of companies have benefited from his training
methods. Richard Denny's uncanny ability of making people
more successful has made him one of the most sought after
speakers for conferences and seminars all over the world.

# SELLING TO WIN

## Tested Techniques for Closing the Sale

## RICHARD DENNY

**KOGAN PAGE**

First published in 1988 by
Kogan Page Limited
120 Pentonville Road
London N1 9JN

Reprinted 1988, 1989, 1991, 1992 (twice)

Photoset in North Wales by
Derek Doyle & Associates, Mold, Clwyd
Printed in England by Clays Ltd, St Ives plc

*British Library Cataloguing in Publication Data*

Denny, Richard
  Selling to win.
  1 Salesmanship – Manuals
  I. Title
  658.8′ 5

  ISBN 1-85091-626-0
  ISBN 1-85091-687-X Pbk

# Contents

To Linda, my wife, best friend and business partner,
who sold me on writing this book.

*Nothing happens anywhere in the world until a sale takes place.*
*And salespeople bring in the money that everyone else can eventually live off.*

My grateful thanks to Sally Mudge, a star PA in the 20 category

# Introduction

The purpose of writing this book is to provide at long last a common sense, businesslike and professional approach to training and developing people in the world's greatest profession.

Most business managers agree that it is very difficult to find professional salespeople who can go out and bring back the business. And the real star professionals are, of course, even rarer.

Business people in the United Kingdom have devalued selling for far too long. British managers have convinced themselves that they would do better if they didn't employ salespeople. And, anyhow, good products sell themselves, don't they? Salespeople just demand new cars and fiddle their expense accounts. The buying public, too, have never appreciated the value of salespeople — pushy people with turned-up toes (from all the slammed doors), and funny expressions. Who in their right mind would invite a salesperson round for tea?

Salespeople try never to admit that they are involved in selling. They call themselves 'executives', 'consultants' and 'inspectors'. But nowadays nearly everyone is involved in selling at some level. Doctors, solicitors, estate agents, surveyors, architects, advertising agents — the list is nearly endless — are all looking for new business and have to sell themselves and their services into it.

The world has become more competitive and in order to survive and make progress we all need to understand selling and persuasion. If companies are going to make it into the twentieth century they will need people who are hired to sell. And if they are going to beat the competition, these people will have to be true professionals. This book will show you how to be a professional.

In the first chapter I state my belief that everybody is born with a natural ability to sell. This does not mean that everybody is, or will be, or can be, a professional salesperson. I believe that the foundation is there but the skills must be taught.

I am not promising amazing new techniques that will close every sale. But I do promise that if you follow me you will

- master the art of selling
- be a true professional
- be recognised by your colleagues as a WINNER and a STAR.

You will frequently find yourself saying 'Yes, I know *that*' or 'Yes, *that* isn't particularly new.' You may *know* it, but do you *do* it? This book shows you how to do it.

Consider this old saying:

*A good salesperson can sell anything.*

It is rubbish. A good salesperson can only sell *anything* if he or she believes in it. Product belief is *essential*. Product knowledge is important, but not as important as enthusiasm.

As a business consultant I am often asked to go into a client company and teach their salespeople how to sell X. Now, if I have not sold their product or service myself, and sold it successfully, I believe that I am unqualified to teach them how to sell it. But what I *can* do is to teach those salespeople how to persuade their customers or potential customers to do business with them. *Selling to Win* will do the same job for you. It cannot teach you product knowledge, however vital such knowledge may be. It *will* teach you to exploit the one thing you and I do have totally in common, the market-place. And that market-place is made up of individuals, and buyers. Over the years I have tried very hard to sell to companies, shops, factories, industrial sites, businesses and homes and have *never once* been able to conclude a sale with any one of them. You see, I have only ever been able to make a sale to another *person.*

*Other people* make up our business universe. Now I do agree that at times the question of whether they are really alive or dead arises. We may even wish to use the mirror breath test on some customers. But you can breathe life into your market. Your power to communicate your enthusiasm, not your knowledge, is the key to your success.

## ◀ HOW TO GET MAXIMUM RESULTS ▶ FROM THIS BOOK

As you read this book use a highlighter pen to mark the ideas that appeal to you most, and re-read these regularly. Dip into Chapter 3 and Chapter 16 at least once every two months, and for those of you who believe that the finest investment you will ever make is in yourself, invest from time to time in further motivational books and audio cassettes. Richard Denny (PO Box 16, Moreton-in-Marsh, Gloucestershire GL56 0NH) can supply you with a list of recommended titles.

The *Professional Selling* audio cassette library can be played in your car. Use your travelling time as *learning* time.

‘      W I S E     W O R D S      ’

Selling is a profession and must have recognised professional ethics. The professional spirit seeks professional integrity from pride not compulsion. The professional spirit detects its own violations and penalises them.

Henry Ford, 1922

# 1

# Selling in Perspective

A great deal of nonsense is talked about selling and the people involved in it. There is also a great deal of justified frustration among disillusioned customers. So let me begin by clarifying some of the misconceptions before highlighting the genuine customer grievances.

◀ *THE CLASSIC CLOSE* ▶

Selling in all honesty has to be the oldest profession. Yet still to this day there are many people who argue forcibly that some people are *natural* salespeople. I actually believe that everybody is born a salesperson, and some go on to develop their skills and later become true professionals. Consider the following scenario.

A father is out shopping with his young child:
'Daddy can I have an ice-cream please?'

The father replies:

'No, you can't right now, because if you eat an ice-cream you won't eat lunch.'

Does the child reply, 'Fine. I quite understand that. Never mind, I'll ask again after lunch if that's alright daddy?'

No. Almost certainly the child says, 'I want an ice-cream.'

The parent replies: 'No, you can't have one. I've just told you.'

The child asks again: 'Please daddy I want my ice-cream.'

'You're not having one. I've made up my mind, and that's all there is to it.'

The child now proceeds with his closing technique. He lies on the floor, kicks his feet in the air and screams 'I want an ice-cream. I want an ice-cream.'

The desperate parent instantly purchases the ice-cream and hands it to the child saying, 'Here you are, but don't tell mummy.'

This is the classic sales presentation. The child exhibits one of the great qualities of professional salesmanship which is, of course, persistence. Even more important, however, is the fact that he does not accept the word 'NO'. Now, I am not suggesting that in order to transact the business the salesperson should lie down on the prospective customer's floor screaming at the top of his voice that he wants the order. It might work, but it would also build an extraordinary reputation!

◀ ## 'NO NO CONDITIONING' ▶

So now let's see what happens to our young super salesman.

The child grows and during his formative years, he is groomed and, sadly, brainwashed by what can best be described as 'No No Conditioning'. The child begins to understand the full implications of the word, 'NO'.

He leaves school, college or university, and makes his way

into the world with aspirations in many cases diminished, expectations curtailed and, in the vast majority of cases, a feeling that he can't ASK because of the subconscious fear of the word 'NO'. This is perceived as a rejection. (Imagine for a minute an unreal world where the word 'NO' does not exist. What would YOU be asking for each and every day?)

There are thousands of so-called salespeople who to this day are still conditioned and brainwashed by total fear of this word, 'NO'. They become a disgrace to themselves, their families and their profession because they are unable to bring themselves to *ask* for the business, the order, the brief, the contract.

## ◀ WHAT NOT TO DO WHEN THE ▶ CUSTOMER SAYS 'NO'

Until we have *asked*, we salespeople are already in a 'NO' situation. If the worse thing any prospective customer can say is 'NO' it really isn't too bad. I much prefer to have the NOs coming through. They can cut out a great deal of wasted follow-up time and effort, because far too many salespeople get trapped in the proverbial pipeline situation, 'there is a lot of business in the pipe'. Many weak salespeople build too big a pipeline of sales that *might* materialise. Much of this business never actually gets closed off. It just drifts away because of the fear of asking for the order.

If a customer says 'NO' you should persist, but *relax*. After all, you can't win them all. It is highly unlikely that we will ever produce a selling technique which will help the seller to close every sale. Of course, we have all seen the sales course brochures and the books which offer the ULTIMATE, the FINAL, and the MOST EFFECTIVE, NEW method of persuading the customer to submit. There are apparently more than one hundred ways of closing a sale. You could use the Half Nelson technique, for instance, or, if you are facing a particularly tricky prospect, a Full Nelson. The trouble with such techniques is that you need, first of all, an amazing memory to recall them and, secondly, some outstanding decision-making skills to decide which one to use!

But in reality this approach is completely out of date.

People nowadays are far better educated, more discerning and have a greater choice than ever before. And the problem with so much sales training has been that the salesperson has been trained to assume that if 'You say this, the customer will say that'.

One problem is that *customers* have never been trained. The buying public is certainly less gullible in some countries. Furthermore, there is a great misconception that in order to be good at selling, one has to have 'the gift of the gab' or 'a bit of the Blarney'. Well, do *you* like to buy from a wind-em-up, shoot-em-out-of-the-door, fast-talking, gift-of-the-gab smoothie? No, and neither does anybody else.

Another serious misconception is that salespeople must have a sales spiel or patter. And again, sadly, many prospective sellers go on some course or other and are taught the sales spiel. It is a set-piece presentation and, in many cases, it is learnt parrot fashion.

But after the course the prospective seller confronts a potential customer and launches this sales spiel! Do you know when somebody is sales spieling you? Of course you do, and so does the buying public. Sales spiels should not be a part of professional selling.

But people actually *like buying*! And they appreciate being sold to well. That is the art of the professional seller. Create an atmosphere that is enjoyable for the customer. I love being sold to well. I despise those who believe that they are salespeople but who do the job unprofessionally, only worsening the image that, sadly, in some cases is deserved.

# ◀ WHAT ARE BAD SALESPEOPLE LIKE? ▶

There is now no longer any excuse for companies to send out poorly trained salespeople. Poorly trained sellers, for one thing, are certainly much more costly to employ.

Most companies claim that 80 per cent of their business comes in from 20 per cent of the salespeople. This '80:20 ratio' is actually a normal distribution curve and one can apply the 80:20 rule to almost anything, but in the sales environment the 80 per cent not only fail to attract business for their employer, they also create intense customer disillusionment or frustration.

## THE ORDER-TAKER

Who are these salespeople? First of all there is the 'classic' salesperson who is no more than an order-taker. For years, the British car industry was in the fortunate position of having a greater demand than supply. You would go to a showroom, search out a so-called salesperson and proceed to show an interest in a particular model. If you had a vehicle to part exchange it would be given a cursory inspection and insulted. The 'salesperson' would kick the tyres and tell you, with much head-shaking and cheek-sucking that your particular vehicle would be 'impossible to sell'. It would almost certainly be the wrong colour and, of course, that particular model did not hold its value.

So, thoroughly dejected, you would agree terms and ask to be put on the waiting list for the car of your choice. You would probably have to wait for six months or a year, to get a new car.

Then, almost overnight, supply seemed to be outpacing demand and suddenly the so-called salesperson (order-taker) was called upon to *sell*, even to this day many showrooms exhibit very out-of-date models — the sales staff!

So, how do you get the customer to say YES? Easy, be professional.

## ◀ HOW DO I BECOME A ▶ PROFESSIONAL?

During the last World War there was a soldier who, when promoted to the rank of general, discovered that he was the youngest man in history ever to be promoted so far. So, quite naturally, he felt very proud and honoured but, equally, very concerned. He explained to his wife his concern about whether or not he was up to the job and if he would have the respect not only of his peers but also of his subordinates. His wife gave him some extremely sound advice:

'Think like a general. Speak like a general. Look like a general. Act like a general ... And you will *be* a general.'

There could be no better advice to anyone who wishes to be recognised as a true sales professional.

Think, speak, look and act like a professional salesman and you will be one.

## ◀ WHAT DO SALES PROFESSIONALS ▶ DO?

Professional salespeople help customers to make buying decisions. They close the sale.

I was taught a great principle by the first (and only) sales manager that I ever had to report to. His name was Barry Wells and he was a great motivator. He wrote in huge letters on a blackboard at my first training sessions, KISS. It stands for, 'Keep It Simple Stupid'. I had it drummed into me to keep my record systems, my operating methods and my presentations simple, and I suggest that when you are in doubt you should choose the simple way. As you go through this book you will find that my thoughts about winning business and closing sales are always simple. They are easy to use but I can guarantee that they work.

So, what do sales professionals do? They keep it simple.

**'**        W I S E    W O R D S        **'**

Show me a successful person and I will show you a salesman. The fact is we are all selling one way or another.

Richard Denny

# 2

# *Planning to Win*

◀ ## *THE SIX CYLINDERS OF PROFESSIONAL SELLING* ▶

Throughout the world nearly all salesmen are interested in motor cars. So I will, from time to time, use the motor car as the basis of an analogy. If you happen to own a thoroughbred six cylinder vehicle you will know that for peak performance, to ensure that you are first away and first at the finish, all cylinders must be running smoothly. So let's create the six cylinders of a professional salesperson.

1. Business knowledge
2. Industry knowledge
3. Company knowledge
4. Product knowledge
5. Sales skills
6. Attitude

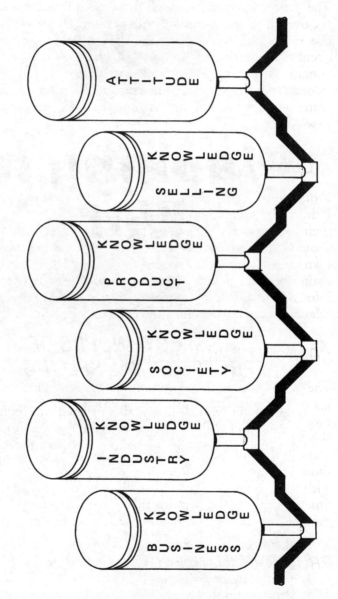

Figure 1   The six cylinders of a professional salesperson

## BUSINESS KNOWLEDGE

The professional salesperson must be fully up-to-date with the overall business climate both at home and overseas. He or she should be well-read, should be able to converse with clients on marketing trends, on changes in the business climate and on home and international politics. This information comes, of course, from listening to the radio, watching television and from reading magazines and newspapers.

## INDUSTRY KNOWLEDGE

Professional salespeople must be fully informed about the industry of which they are part. They should be familiar with their competitors' products, prices and positioning. They should be aware of other people or personalities within their own industry, and they should be aware of their competitors' main selling points and new product releases. This information is readily available in the trade press and from relevant societies, organisations and professional bodies.

## COMPANY KNOWLEDGE

The professional salesperson must be a good ambassador for his or her company, which means that they should be well aware of company policy, in-company schedules. They should be particularly well informed about their company's marketing and advertising programmes and lastly, they should know the right people and departmental contacts within the organisation. This will, of course, mean that from time to time they can point their own customer or client in the right direction for assistance or further business.

## PRODUCT KNOWLEDGE

That you should know your product thoroughly may seem obvious, but it is quite extraordinary how many salespeople are not fully conversant with the products that they are attempting to sell. Nothing is more frustrating for customers than salespeople who are ignorant about their products. But, perhaps even more importantly, if you don't have a profound knowledge of your product you will be unable to exercise *any* persuasive skills. You will show a lack of *belief*, and in the end you will inevitably join the 80 per cent we met in Chapter 1.

So, if you have been asked to sell a product or service and you have not been provided with any training on that product or service, it is up to you as a professional salesperson to ask the questions that will satisfy your professionalism. Let me state quite emphatically here that having the most knowledge about a particular product does not mean that you will win the most business. Like almost everything in life, the balance has to be right and product knowledge without sales skills is most certainly not the recipe for success.

But you as a salesperson must be credible. You must be able to convince your client that what you are selling will be right for him or her.

Two classic cases of salespeople failing to be credible spring to mind. My wife and I wished to purchase a new dishwasher recently. We were in a white goods retailer and were faced with a choice of six manufacturers and various models. Four different assistants were unable to outline the advantages or disadvantages of any one machine! They had no idea of why there was such price variation other than that they were from different manufacturers!

Example number two: we decided to purchase a further property and we asked the selling estate agent what I considered to be very normal questions for prospective purchasers — whether or not the property had gas, for instance. We then spent the next 20 minutes searching to see if the property had gas! We also wanted to know who owned the boundary fences, hedges and walls and exactly where the boundaries were. But the agent had to check with the client.

These were simple questions which any professional salesperson should have been able to answer instantly.

There will obviously be times when the best informed salespeople are caught out by a question which they have never been asked before. In those circumstances it is, of course, quite in order to apologise to the client and give him or her the information as soon as you have the answers. But this should be the *exception*, not the rule.

## SALES SKILLS

Even those of you who have been in sales for many years will agree that from time to time you forget the basic rules of professional selling. You may know them but are you operating by those rules? The sheer pressure of the current business climate causes many good salespeople to get themselves into a rut or a 'comfort zone'. They forget to use the sales skills that they learned many years previously.

The greater part of this book will, of course, be discussing these in depth.

## ATTITUDE

This is, of course, the ultimate characteristic that distinguishes the star professional in the 20 per cent category from the 'also rans'. Throughout this book we will be discussing numerous ideas to make sure you always have the correct, positive attitude.

Now let's return to the motor car analogy. All owners from time to time take their vehicle to a garage for a service. They do this because they know that unless the engine has all cylinders running smoothly, their vehicle will eventually let them down. It is really quite extraordinary that so many professional people are not adopting the six cylinder philosophy. May I suggest to you that at least once a month you check your six cylinders: is each one running smoothly?

Or has a cylinder become worn and pitted or, worst of all, seized up?

*Knowledge is power*, we are told. In fact, in the world of professional selling, knowledge is potential power. We all get paid for *using* our knowledge, not for just knowing. '*It's not what you know that matters, it's who you know that really matters*,' we are told. But that, of course, is not strictly true either. It's *what* you do with who you know that really matters.

◄   **WHAT DO YOU LOOK LIKE?**   ►

What, in the outward appearance of a person who is selling to *you*, gives you a feeling of confidence and trust? I am sure you will say that there is no absolute rule, and I agree. So let's go to the principle rather than the specific. The professional salesperson should *look the part*, and by looking the part they should conform to their industry type. If you are in the financial sector your appearance should, of course, be of a more conservative nature yet, at the same time, projecting an image of success. The clothes should be smart, you should look well-groomed and you should pay particular attention to shoes. If, however, you were involved in the agricultural industry, selling to farmers, or suppliers, your appearance would, of course, need to be completely different. There are always exceptions and I am sure you will be able to point to at least one person who breaks these principles and yet is a star performer. But never base your future, your income, your success on the exception to the rule. If you want to be a true professional, make sure that you look good, and always give the impression of success. People would rather do business with a success than a failure, a drop-out or a has-been. I continually preach that the greatest investment *anyone* can make is in oneself, but much more about that later.

You should apply the same principle to anything that you

as the seller might present to a customer. Sales aids, brochures and presentation files must all have a professional image. It is up to you to replace them when they start to become tatty. A lot of buying is based upon gut feelings, emotion and first impressions. In selling the old cliché that it is the first impression that really counts, *really counts.*

◀  ## ORGANISATION TACTICS  ▶

The third stage of preparation is the organisation of the professional salesperson's business activity.

Salespeople should really approach their jobs as though they are running their own business. You may be an employee or you may be self-employed, but you should regard selling as an opportunity to run a business. The employer and the employer's products or services are an umbrella, and underneath that umbrella it is the duty of the professional salesperson to make the most of the opportunities that arise.

◀  ## KEEPING GOOD RECORDS  ▶

Chapter 4 covers time management and organisation, but at this stage of our preparation let's make sure that you, the professional seller, have got the system right in order to maximise your time but also never to lose out on potential business that may be months, or even years away.

One of the most successful sales managers in the UK is Bill Jack, now the marketing manager of the giant General Accident Corporation. He has always operated a two-diary system for his sales business — one for this year and one for next. This year's diary is, of course, used for listing his appointments, his calls, and his meetings but next year's diary is used for anniversary dates of important clients, dates for follow-up visits, dates for recalls and dates for client contacts.

It is, of course, extremely motivational to see at the beginning of the year the possibilities of business in advance. But just as importantly, it is extremely effective to be able to mail a card in time for an anniversary, or phone to wish a valued customer a happy birthday.

Clive Holmes on the other hand, perhaps the UK's most outstandingly successful professional in the life insurance industry, uses his time and his record keeping as part of his long-term business strategy. In itself, this almost becomes a closing technique in its own right. Clive states that when in discussion with a new prospect, he will ask his client: 'Are you prepared to give up two hours of your time once a year to allow me to review your financial affairs? Because if you are not prepared to do that, I can't service your business correctly.' The client quite naturally agrees to such an arrangement and the business at that stage is closed. Clive is able to record a further meeting one year from that date. He is a true professional, looking for long-term business in the very best interest of his client.

## CUSTOMER SERVICE

The most valuable item I have in my office is my customer list. My building could be destroyed, I could lose all my money, investments and property, but if I am left with my client list, I will be back in business within hours. Far too few salespeople attach sufficient importance to their client list. This is one of the great weaknesses of British commercial life.

One of the most striking examples of an industry which undervalues its customer base is provided by the building societies. I can think of no independent business person who could ignore their best customers and stay in business as consistently as the building societies. The best customers a building society has are its borrowers, those people to whom

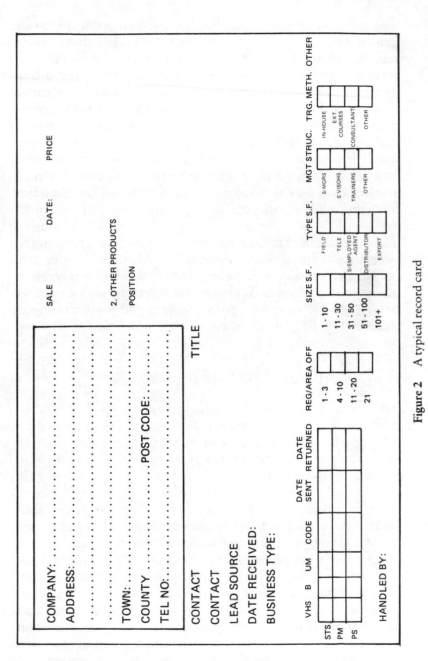

**Figure 2**  A typical record card

they have sold a mortgage. The building society will entirely ignore those customers throughout the period that regular repayments are kept up, except that once a year they will send them a statement and perhaps also a circular announcing profits. But they do nothing else for those excellent customers. Of course, if borrowers should fall behind with repayments, then suddenly the building society will take a great interest in them. And so we have seen the financial institutions moving in to sell their products to the building societies' superb customer base. In many cases customers are paying more for financial services than they would have done if they had bought them from the building society!

As I write, the building societies are just awakening to the enormous value of their customer list. There is a lesson here for all professional salespeople. Keep detailed information about your customers. Whether you store this on a computer or a very basic card index filing system you must record the information. Keep it and use it.

## A TYPICAL RECORD CARD

You can keep all your client information on one card. On the reverse side of the card record each meeting or conversation and points of detail that can be used later. But, like all information, it is only of real value as long as it is kept up-to-date. (See Figure 2.)

As a professional you must be able to judge your performance with individual clients. This leads to the quite natural desire to judge one's overall performance, and to analyse one's sales closing ratio. You must *exact* information, numbers of leads to numbers of appointments, and numbers of sales to numbers of appointments. With this information, the professional salesperson can clearly identify the areas that may require additional effort. Is it the quality of leads that have to be improved? Maybe a better appointment-setting technique? Perhaps the weakness even lies in an inability to close the sales. You can only act on these problems if you

**Monthly Sales Analysis**    From:    For:

| Appointments made by | This month | Cum totals |
|---|---|---|
| Telesales | | |
| Marketing | | |
| Self | | |
| Adv | | |
| Other | | |
| Totals | | |

| | Sales this month | | Cum totals | | Conversion rate | |
|---|---|---|---|---|---|---|
| | No. | Value | No. | Value | App/Sales | £/App |
| | | | | | | |
| | | | | | | |
| | | | | | | |
| | | | | | | |
| | | | | | | |

**Top ten for (month)**

| Customer | Course | Value |
|---|---|---|
| | | |
| | | |
| | | |
| | | |

**Sales this month**

| Customer | Lead time | Project | Value |
|---|---|---|---|
| | | | |
| | | | |
| | | | |
| | | | |

Figure 3   Sample month's sales analysis

33

**Weekly Activity Report**   From:   For:

| Day/Date | Client | Activity | Comment | Sold | £ Value |
|---|---|---|---|---|---|
|  |  |  |  |  |  |

Figure 4   Sample weekly activity report

have first rate information systems. Figure 3 shows a monthly sales analysis. Such a document, designed to your own sales activities, can make you a lot of money. It is developed from the weekly activity report (Figure 4) and requires neither immense intellectual nor physical effort to complete. Both will repay you handsomely if you use the information intelligently.

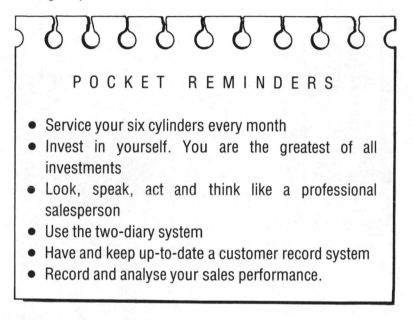

POCKET REMINDERS

- Service your six cylinders every month
- Invest in yourself. You are the greatest of all investments
- Look, speak, act and think like a professional salesperson
- Use the two-diary system
- Have and keep up-to-date a customer record system
- Record and analyse your sales performance.

**'**    W I S E   W O R D S    **'**

The person who gets ahead is the one who does more than is necessary and keeps on doing it.

Richard Denny

# 3

# The Vital Ingredient

There is one characteristic that separates the star salesperson of the world from the rest. There is one characteristic that separates the great sportsperson of the world from the rest. There is one characteristic that distinguishes the winners from the losers. And that is ATTITUDE.

◀ *THE VITAL INGREDIENT* ▶

Over years of running hundreds of sales courses, I have been asked by many managers to try and pick up the strengths and weaknesses of their delegates and to pick out the salespeople who are going to make it. I am often asked to judge people on their performance on sales courses. My response has, and always will be, to judge by *results* only.

A delegate on a sales course can perform admirably, have all the right answers and appear to be totally committed.

However, this does *not* mean that this is the individual who will be the winner out in the market-place. At all my courses, I talk about the circle of success. This circle breaks down into two parts: PRODUCT KNOWLEDGE on the one part, and SELLING SKILLS on the other.

A salesman may know all about his product, he may know all the sales skills from the beginning of time, he may know every closing technique ever dreamt up but this does *not* mean he will be a champion. Because ATTITUDE alone is the vital ingredient that all the stars have totally in common.

So WHAT is the right attitude?

It is possibly best summed up as a deep-down, unshakeable conviction that you *will* win. It is having a truly positive attitude of mind. And a positive attitude of mind is again perhaps most easily defined as always looking for the best, and *expecting* to win. It is being optimistic. It's being faced with any given situation and being able to look on the bright side, seeing what might lead to a positive result and not a negative one.

People have said to me, 'You can't teach a positive attitude of mind.' This is ridiculous. You CAN teach anything. What I am sure is really being said to me is that people can't learn to build a positive attitude of mind. They are saying that some are born with it and others are not. I find this completely unacceptable and ridiculous.

Our attitudes of mind are very much based on life's experiences — our conditioning in childhood, the company we keep, and the environment we work and play in. Individuals *can* change an attitude of mind if they want to, if they are given the greatest gift that any human being can give to another, and that is to teach the difference between the positive and the negative.

So HOW have the truly positive people, the winners, the stars and the champions, built their own positive attitude? It stems from learning the philosophies of success and principles upon which they base their actions and faults. In many cases, these principles and philosophies have had to be adopted against all odds and against a great deal of past negative conditioning.

I now want to run through ten winning ideas that make up the vital ingredient.

## ◀ 1 IT'S DESIRE, NOT ABILITY THAT ▶ DETERMINES SUCCESS

Many people question their ability — 'I can't', or, 'I am unable to', 'I haven't had enough experience', 'I haven't the right education', 'I didn't go to the right schools', or, 'I'm not the lucky sort'. Some even go as far as to say, 'I wasn't born to the right parents', 'I wasn't born under the right birthsign.'

LET ME say to YOU, *you* can do *anything* you really want to. If you want to do something badly enough, whether you have the ability or not has nothing to do with it. It is *how badly* you want to do it.

We have all seen the example of young people leaving school without qualifications. They might be unemployed or they might take a temporary job. Suddenly they find a career they want to get into but need some qualifications. So they go back into a place of learning and retake the exams that previously they had failed dismally. But this time they pass. WHY? Has their *ability* changed? No, of course not. But their DESIRE *has* changed.

Now let me give you a simple example: I invite you to join a new company I have just created. We are going to go out and sell a new calculator. The selling price will be £45. For each one that you sell, you will get £10 commission. Do YOU think you could sell 300 in the first three months?

Now, if you are thinking quite naturally, 'No I am not sure I could do that', or even more emphatically, 'No I can't do that', let me try something else: 'If YOU sell 300 of these calculators during the next three months I will give you £100,000 but you can't buy any yourself.' What would you say now?

YES, positively, 'Of course I can do that.' But what has that got to do with your ability to sell calculators?

What this simple example shows is that a change of attitude can bring about an outstanding change of result. One or two of you may have thought you would be smart and you would sell them all to a relation. If confronted with that sort of opportunity you can always find a short cut or a short and easy answer. But I am quite certain you get the message I am really making here: EVERY ONE of us has the ability to do better; EVERY ONE of us CAN, if we REALLY want to.

There is an expression that says *Don't be so heavenly minded you are no earthly good.* POSITIVE THINKING, like anything else, can be carried too far. It will not move mountains but it WILL move the individual.

There are some people who might say, 'I want to be a world record breaking hundred metre sprinter.' If they haven't got the basic physique or frame upon which to build the muscle, they are being unrealistic. If they are far too old, they are being unrealistic. If they fall into either of these two categories, I question whether they *really, really* want to be a world record beater in sprinting. However, in all reality, there are some people who are born with sheer genius, so there is always an exception to the rule. DON'T EVER base your income or your future on exceptions because there is an exception that will disprove the point.

Let me ask you these questions. HOW STRONG is your desire? HOW BADLY do you want to win? HOW DETERMINED are you to be a success in selling?

If you feel that your desire is lacking, you must now proceed to my second idea.

◀  ## 2  SET YOUR GOALS  ▶

There is a well known cliché that says, 'A person going nowhere, normally gets there'. So if you find your desire is not as strong as it should be, it is possible you have not firmly set out the goals you want to achieve. Perhaps your personal motivation is lacking. I have seen numerous examples of people who appear not to have had the talent, skills or ability, yet they become outstanding successes in their own right and within their own field. And the one thing they all have in common is that they were deeply *motivated* towards their *goals* and *objectives* in life.

The great Andrew Carnegie was quoted as saying, 'Give me a man of average ability but a burning desire and I will give you a winner in return every time.' So now follow these simple steps in deciding your goals and building your desire and motivation.

Put aside one weekend when you and your partner, or if you are single, on your own, will decide exactly what it is you really want. Draw up a list of everything both long and short term, both tangible and intangible in your business life, in your private life, in your social life, and for your hobbies and

| Goal Chart  Goals I really want | |
| --- | --- |
| Exact business goals | Date |
| Exact personal goals | Date |
| Exact family goals | Date |
| Exact social and hobby goals | Date |

**Figure 5**  A goal chart

pastimes. Then, in each category decide what is the first goal you are going for. You must be able to achieve this goal WITHIN THREE MONTHS. Make it too far away and your motivation will not be strong enough. Whatever you do, DON'T make this goal too high.

Many ill-informed teachers of success stress you must set yourself big goals and aim high. The basic premise is, of course, correct — reaching high can broaden one's thinking. It's sound advice but they fail to back it up by teaching one of the rules of success, that cliché which says, '*Success by the inch is a cinch but by the yard it is hard*'. If you set too big a goal you will have difficulty in believing you will achieve it — if you don't believe it, you are making its achievement virtually impossible.

Large goals are therefore best broken down into a series of realistically managed stages. This now leads on to another of those success laws which says, '*Seeing ourselves progressing, motivates us*'. You have all heard it voiced in the expression 'Success breeds success'. Don't fight these rules and laws, USE them. Equally, don't break them.

The human brain is a goal-seeking mechanism, as mankind's incredible developments have proved. Programme your mind towards achieving goals; give your mind and brain a chance to perform with some objectives to aim for. You *will* become more creative and more constructive when you aim at a firmly defined objective that you want at all costs.

Having now drawn up your list of goals, set a firm date for achieving them. As I have already said, a human being ALWAYS responds to deadlines. With that first goal, make sure you have a clear and complete picture of exactly what it is you are going for. The brain and the mind must be pointed in the correct direction with a clearly defined end-result. Losing weight by the end of June may sound like a goal for somebody putting themselves on a diet but it is not. They should state exactly what weight they want their body to be by the end of June.

Somebody who says they want to be the star salesman that year should decide exactly what it is that makes up the star salesman. Break the target down into a series of monthly achievements with a clearly defined goal per month. Another person might say she wants a new car. She decides the date but perhaps she hasn't decided the model, make, colour, price and all the extras she wants with it.

I said earlier that it is of paramount importance for those of you who have a partner to discuss your goals together. The preparation of your goal list has very little to do with anyone else other than your partner! Two people pulling together in the same direction become an unbeatable force. Two people living together with separate goals could be a recipe for disaster.

The final stage of goal setting is to write your goals down and have them readily available. I personally write my goals in my diary as soon as I get it in the New Year. You might find it more pertinent to put them on a large sheet of paper on the wall. REMEMBER, a weekend spent planning the future and deciding your goals and objectives, will not be wasted. This should be your own personal master plan.

# ◀  *3 PLANNING YOUR GOALS*  ▶

IT MAY be rather unusual to put this heading under what is obviously a chapter on principles and philosophies of success, but just as planning is important for your business options, equally so is goal setting. If you are now going to do exactly as I have suggested, the next stage is to plan each goal.

For the captain of an aircraft flying from London to New York the destination is his goal. The achievement of that goal will very much depend upon his plan. As soon as he takes the aircraft off the runway, he will be working on his flight plan which he'll check continually throughout the flight. None of us hope we will ever be unfortunate enough to be taken into the air by a captain who has no flight plan, yet there are salespeople who are continually launched into the world with set targets, but who fail to map out their plans.

Success very rarely happens by CHANCE. It is PLANNED.

Jealous individuals commenting on other people's achievements may well say, 'Oh they're just lucky.' SUCCESSFUL people will often attribute their success to just being lucky —they are of course just being extremely modest. Luck is aptly defined by the following mnemonic:

> Labour
> Under
> Correct
> Knowledge

LABOUR, of course, means work or effort. The CORRECT KNOWLEDGE is knowing where you are today, knowing where you are going (goals in mind) and with a plan to get there. CHANCE is a win on a lottery, the premium bond number that comes up, or the win on the football pools. DON'T leave your future to chance. MAKE yourself lucky.

## The Plan For Each Goal

The goal must now be broken down into a series of believable and easily manageable stages.

**What do I need to do?**                    **Date**

1.

2.

3.

4.

5.

6.

7.

8.

9.

10.

**Figure 6**   A goal plan

◀          *4 BELIEVE IN YOU*          ▶

You must believe in you because if you don't nobody else will! More importantly, if you believe in you, that you CAN, you are already building a positive attitude of mind.

Don't say, 'I can't', as this is a dangerous negative which is being actively fed into the most valuable assets any human being has — the brain, the mind, the thinking process. Far too few people value these great assets. Surely the greatest investment people can make is to invest in themselves, because it is only themselves who will provide for the whole of their life and who will provide for their loved ones. Isn't it extraordinary how few people will spend money in that direction!

People with cars regularly spend up to £150 to have them serviced. They feel that if they don't, it will let them down or will not run properly. To prevent the misery of a vehicle that gives up on them and a long walk to the telephone (that probably won't be working), people send their cars in to have this regular service carried out. How many friends of yours will take themselves along to a course to learn some new ideas, as well as some old? How many friends do you know who regularly spend £100 on buying motivational cassettes, videos or books?

They take their greatest asset for granted. At worst they don't even bother to think that it might need revitalising from time to time, that it does get tired, that it does forget, and that it does fail to deliver at peak performance. If nothing else, DO PICK UP THIS BOOK AND READ THIS CHAPTER AT LEAST EVERY SIX MONTHS. Then turn to the last chapter in this book to make sure you haven't caught the most evil, dangerous, cancerous complaint humanity has ever inflicted upon itself.

Whenever the brain is fed the command instruction, 'I can't', it will respond by thinking of ways that it can't. It becomes active in thinking of new ways to prove that it can't, until finally it comes up with ways it can't that it has never thought of before!

On the other hand, when it is given the command, 'I can', it will quickly respond to becoming creative and to thinking of ways that it CAN.

Again, let's be realistic about bringing the balance between downright stupid goals and those that are realistically obtainable. Through past experiences or conditioning you may have to remove what I can best describe as false ceilings in the mind. These arise from past failures or negative experiences but you must catch yourself saying, 'I can't' or, 'I'm not even going to try because I tried that before and it didn't work then, so I am not going to try again now.'

## BELIEF IN ONESELF IS ONE OF THE GREATEST MOTIVATORS.

The well-documented story of Dr. Roger Bannister, the first person to break the four minute mile, makes the point very well. It had been said that the human frame was not built in such a way that it could run a mile in less than four minutes. It had never been done before. Bannister knew he could run a quarter-mile in under a minute and he clearly pictured in his mind stringing together those four quarter-miles to such an extent that he knew he could do it. HE BELIEVED IN ROGER BANNISTER. He then broke that world record. Within days other people were running a mile in under four minutes! They built their own belief in themselves because they knew that if he could do it, so could they.

There is nothing wrong in this philosophy, but there are times when you will have to be the pioneer — when you will have to be the Roger Bannister. However, by setting the goal and by planning its achievement, you will be giving yourself a chance to BELIEVE in YOU.

◀ ## 5 BECOME A 'HOW CAN I DO IT ▶
BETTER' SORT OF PERSON

This is the positive characteristic of realising we can all do whatever we do a little better. Some people say, 'I'm doing my best' and of course they truly are at that moment. But whenever we say 'I'm doing my best' we are equally indicating that we can't improve. So don't put a false ceiling, a barrier, in the path of your growth.

So many people react negatively towards change, 'Why change it, that's the way it's always been done?' I am not saying change for the sake of change. Mary Kaye Ash, that brilliant entrepreneurial president of Mary Kaye cosmetics, states, *'If it works, don't fix it'*. This is a sound principle.

I am referring to the natural human characteristic of the fear of change, the fear of uncertainty, the fear of the unknown, that causes a negative reaction. The positive person is always looking for improvement both in their actions and the scope of their thinking. Business managers often say to me, 'Richard, how do you judge a person?' And my reply is, 'By the size of their thinking.'

A truly positive person concentrates on the principles, and *always* expects to be able to do better.

◀ ## 6 SEE THE OAK TREE IN THE ACORN ▶

It is so easy in life just to see the acorn and not the oak tree. In your relationships with customers or prospects, try and see what MIGHT be as against what APPEARS to be.

In 1974, I jointly formed a company with my good friend, Robin Fielder. The company was to be called Leadership Development. We needed some brochures to be printed outlining our services, and we naturally called in some printers to quote for the job.

One particular printer asked how many brochures we would need. When we told him five hundred he looked down his nose, pulled himself up to his full height, and with an air of disdain, informed us with all the self-importance he could muster that his firm didn't even start the machines for a run of five hundred. He then went on to make Robin and me feel very small and very insignificant.

Some two years later, due to the growth of our business our print run was now running between 500,000 and 1,000,000 pieces a time! Would you believe it? That same printer returned to our offices one day and I believe he had actually forgotten he had ever met us before. He came in smarmily and creepily, hoping to close a sale. I think it must have been one of the most satisfying days Robin and I ever had — our chance to turn the tables. We had waited two years for this day, and if ever there were two people who had been given that extra fire in their bellies to prove success, that poor little man was confronted by them. I doubt whether he has ever forgotten that day. He was unable to see the oak tree from the original acorn.

What he should have said at that first meeting was something to this effect, 'Mr Denny and Mr Fielder, I am extremely sorry but at this stage I am unable to give you a price or the service you currently require, but please, later on, when your print runs and requirements are greater, do give me another chance to do business with you'.

A positive attitude is one that always looks for the good points in people rather than the bad points. Try and see what might be as against what appears to be, and always practice the art of adding value to people.

# ◀ *7 DEVELOP THE HABIT OF* ▶ *COMPLIMENTING PEOPLE*

This has to be one of the greatest qualities of true leadership. It takes a big-thinking individual to give another person a compliment.

I am not suggesting you should give a compliment just for the sake of giving a compliment as this can have a negative effect. So many business managers will find fault either with their staff or their colleagues but they far too infrequently congratulate them when they do something right. They tell them, even jump on them, the minute they make a mistake. But we make people grow when we pay them a compliment. In my professional management course, both live and in the video version, I state that simple expression, '*Catch them doing something right*'.

For all of us in the sales world are often dependent on the help and support we get from our colleagues within the office environment. Always give a compliment when a job has been well done, or at the very least a thank you. This positive habit, like every other habit, requires continual practice. Be aware of people around you, open your eyes and notice what's going on.

◀   *8 BUILD YOUR CONFIDENCE*   ▶

It must be remembered that every person progressing through life will from time to time lack confidence.

Confidence in so many instances comes from FAMILI-ARITY. If we are doing something new, it is at that stage that we feel a lack of confidence. A traffic warden in the high streets, checking the parking meters or issuing parking tickets, will almost certainly be very confident. If he or she is about to put a ticket on your car, your excuse will almost certainly have been heard before. Take that traffic warden and ask him or her to make a business presentation to a group of directors in a boardroom, and of course the confidence will disappear.

Before we look at the stages of building confidence, let's explore three types of conditioning we are subjected to.

Firstly, we are conditioned by our environment. That is, the people we mix with, the people we work with and the people we socialise with. People will naturally conform to their environment. If you were to only mix, meet and talk with millionaires, that alone would immeasurably increase your chance of becoming one.

Why do we ensure that children don't get into 'bad company'? Because we know that if they do they will conform to the behaviour of the group. The same can be said of adults.

Secondly, we are conditioned by our childhood. Let's imagine a parent that has decided to paint the living room of the family home. This particular father doesn't really like painting and wants to get the job done as quickly as possible.

His five-year-old child enters the room, picks up a paint brush and proceeds to help his father. Now if the father says, 'Johnny, paint this little corner down here,' shows him what to do and encourages him, the child will do a little bit and, as we all know, will get bored very quickly and trot off out, to go and play with his toys. But that is not what normally happens. The father wanting to get the job done, sees his child entering the room, tells him to run out and play. As we have already said, most five-year-olds do not normally accept NO for an answer. The child picks up the paint brush and starts to have a go. The father snaps again, 'Put that brush down.' But the child is of course completely deaf to the word NO. The father, in final desperation, snatches the brush from Johnny, gives him a tap on the bottom, sends him out of the room and perhaps even straight to his bedroom, to stay there until the job is done.

Ten years later, it may be time to paint that room again. The father thinks, 'I'll get Johnny to help me, he's fifteen and the two of us working on this room will get it finished in no time at all.' He calls Johnny to give some help. But Johnny has got better things to do and doesn't want to know. You see Johnny's subconscious recalls that he doesn't like painting and that painting rooms is a painful experience!

Thirdly, we are conditioned by previous adult experience.

| Success experience | Failure experience |
|:---:|:---:|
| ↓ | ↓ |
| Confidence | Lack of confidence |
| ↓ | ↓ |
| I can | I can't |

Imagine the brain is a storage area. Whatever you put into it you, in turn, will get back out. If you feed into it failure experiences, the I can'ts, that is the reaction you will pull out. On the other hand if you feed into it, I can, that again is what will come back out.

Later in this book you will see how I define failure. I don't believe any human being needs to feed the I can'ts into his or her brain.

Five ways to develop greater confidence.

a)  Get Rid of Excuses

DON'T allow yourself to make excuses for non-performance or non-achievement — I am too old, I am too young, I haven't had the right education, I am never in the right place at the right time, I'm just not lucky, or it's not my fault.

ALWAYS be POSITIVE and say to yourself, these positive affirmatives, the 'I can' and 'I am able'. DON'T TALK YOURSELF DOWN.

b)  Build Your Self-Image

Let me ask you, HOW DO YOU SEE YOURSELF? I hope you are pleased. I hope you are proud of what you see, and I equally hope you see ways of improving. You MUST have a good self-image. You MUST have a pride in yourself. You MUST believe in you. You MUST picture yourself as winning and succeeding. There is that great expression, '*We become what we think about*'.

I once said that in a training session and one smart Alec shouted out, 'But I don't want to be a girl!' But it is true, that we do become what we think about. And how you see yourself is what, in turn, will be manifested to others.

c)  Don't Fear Failure

People are conditioned that failure is something dreadful. It's one of the most negative words of all because it conjures up negative picture imagination. But in order to fail, one has at least had to do something. So many people are caught up with this terrible fear of failure that they actually never do anything, they never try, they never have a go.

So what if you fail? The reaction must be 'Fine, I'll have a go at something else,' and do remember it is impossible to fail at anything until you actually give up!

THE ONLY WAY TO CONQUER FEAR IS TO KEEP DOING THE THING YOU FEAR TO DO

d)  Appearance builds confidence

One of the first outward signs of people who are suffering from a lack of confidence (or may be going through a down spell in their own life) is they let their appearance become shabby. Their clothes start to look a little bit untidy and they don't take much care of their hair.

Have you ever had the unfortunate experience of arriving at an evening event where everybody is dressed in a dinner jacket and you turn up in a lounge suit or day dress? You instantly suffer a lack of confidence. You are the SAME person inside, but your appearance does not conform. The smarter the appearance, the greater will be the confidence. Women know how much better they feel when they have been to the hairdresser or they are wearing a new dress. If you are ever going through a tough spell, to help you rekindle your confidence, invest in yourself. Get the outside looking good and the inside will become good.

e)  Compile A Record of Success

Go back to your earliest memory of success. Get a scrap book and write in and record that success experience. It may be at school, winning a race or getting a very good report. From that beginning, add every success you have ever had up to the present and then continually record in your personal success book every new success story. This alone is a great confidence builder as we all have some successes in life but we so often forget them and only remember the failures. In years to come, when you might be suffering a lack of confidence, take out your personal success story and rekindle the 'I can's' because of what you have done in the past.

◀   *9  HANDLE THE DIFFICULT TIMES*   ▶

When things are going well, life and business are very easy to cope with. It's when things aren't going so well that the positive person must fall back to a philosophy which gets him or her back on line. If you are ever experiencing a lack of confidence and your attitude has become negative, this is often brought on because of expectations which don't materialise or because events in many cases are out of your control. These can bring about feelings of uncertainty or, worse a desperate feeling.

Some time ago, I needed to raise half a million pounds for a new project. We put together our proposals, budgets and forecasts. We employed a financial organisation to put us in touch with suitable lenders. Because the project was new and had no track record, we were continually turned down. It got to the stage where we were running past our deadline. The whole of my business's future depended upon getting this next project underway. And then, when the final organisation turned us down, I recalled a saying taught to me some years earlier:

IN EVERY ADVERSITY THERE IS A SEED OF AN EQUIVALENT OR GREATER BENEFIT

So I started again and went out into the market-place myself. Suddenly, it seemed by a stroke of luck, we found a bank not only willing but also enthusiastic, about our project. We were underway. It turned out that the terms of interest were better than we had been advised to expect and we could achieve before, and our methods of repayment were better than we had hoped for.

So whenever you are faced with a crisis or a worry situation, say to yourself, 'How can I turn this to my advantage?' You will be staggered how many times you can do just that. At the very least, you will learn by an experience. But in all honesty in most cases when applying this philosophy, you will turn that crisis back into your favour.

## ◀ 10 BE ENTHUSIASTIC ▶

This is my final characteristic of a positive person. He or she are always enthusiastic. Enthusiasm is so powerful. It is also so infectious. Enthusiasm in the selling world is irresistible and builds belief in your clients. The examples of the effect of the power of enthusiasm are so numerous this quality MUST NEVER be ignored.

Let me give you just one example. When you were at school, did you look forward to your botany classes or was botany a boring old subject? Yet, the subject of botany has become peak viewing on BBC television because of one man and his enthusiasm. I am, of course, talking about David Bellamy. He lectures on this subject with such enthusiasm and belief.

SO HOW does one become more enthusiastic?

You must understand that it is only strong people who force their actions to control their thoughts, rather than just allowing their thoughts to control their actions. Practise smiling. It's hard to say anything nasty when one is smiling. It is hard to have negative thoughts while one is smiling. It is equally very nice to be in the company of a person who smiles.

Dale Carnegie says, '*Enthusiasm is not just an outward expression but once you acquire it, it constantly works within you.*'

So to become enthusiastic, act enthusiastically; force yourself to become an enthusiast.

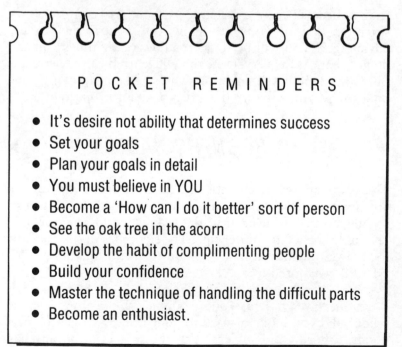

## POCKET REMINDERS

- It's desire not ability that determines success
- Set your goals
- Plan your goals in detail
- You must believe in YOU
- Become a 'How can I do it better' sort of person
- See the oak tree in the acorn
- Develop the habit of complimenting people
- Build your confidence
- Master the technique of handling the difficult parts
- Become an enthusiast.

‘ WISE WORDS ’

The winners in life think constantly in terms of I can, I will and I am. Losers on the other hand concentrate their waking thoughts on what they should have done or what they don't do.

Dennis Waitley

# 4

# *Finding the Time*

We all have an identical bank account, but this bank account has some peculiarities compared to the one that we hold for the management of our finances. You see, with this bank account we can never deposit, we can only withdraw.

With this bank account we can never get a statement. We never know how much we have left in. And with this bank account there is no manager with whom we can discuss the more effective use of it's assets. This, of course, is the bank account of time.

None of us knows how much time we have left available to us and none of us can add more days. So it makes good sense to optimise our time with the overall objective being one of happiness or contentment.

Many business psychologists are researching the causes of stress among executives and these, of course, quite naturally are numerous. My own theory is is that one of the root causes of stress has to be the mismanagement of time. We have all heard people say, there just aren't enough hours in the day. We have all seen friends and colleagues carting home bulging briefcases, and we have all seen the lined faces and drawn expressions of colleagues who are finding that they are not on top of their work. Good time utilisation can prevent a lot of this unhappiness. Think of the most successful person that you know in any given sphere, whether in business, sport, education or politics. What about the most successful salesperson? Get a picture of this individual firmly in your mind. The hard fact is that you have exactly the same hours in the day as that individual. Perhaps their success is a direct result of more efficient time management.

I don't believe anybody has to work a great deal harder to achieve outstanding results. But we can all work that little bit more intelligently. The majority of people work hard anyway. But surely the purpose of work is to provide the income which gives you the opportunity to do the things you enjoy most. Sadly, many people go to work just to fill the hours rather than in order to achieve their goals in life.

There is an enormous difference between activity and achievement. A person can be very busy all day long without actually achieving very much. This sort of person arrives home at the end of the day mentally and physically exhausted, but with little to show for it. Why? The cause is one we have already discussed. These individuals have *not* set themselves clearly defined goals, and they are like ships wallowing in the sea without a rudder. These people suffer from the human frailty of procrastination: they put off things that they should be doing *immediately*.

If you procrastinate, if you get frustrated because there isn't enough time to get everything done, you are not getting the maximum from every moment. The solution is to develop a time organisation system. A whole new industry has grown out of this one idea. But just having or knowing a system is not sufficient. It is only in the *doing* that one is able to be effective. Ask yourself these questions:

- Do you procrastinate
- Do you maximise every day?
- Do you maximise every hour?
- Do you get frustrated because there is not enough time to get everything done?

A few years ago Charles Schwab, who was at that time President of a steel company in the United States, granted an interview to an expert named Ivy Lee. Lee explained his firm's services to Schwab, but Schwab said: 'That's all very well but what we want is more *doing*, not knowing. We already know what should be done. If you can give me a system to help me get more done in the day, I will pay you anything you ask.' Lee replied: 'I'll give you a system. I want you to use it for 30 days and then I want you to get all your key people to use the system for 30 days, and then you send me a cheque for whatever you think it is worth. This idea will only take me a few minutes to explain to you.' A few months later Lee received a cheque for $25,000, with a note from Schwab acknowledging that this was the finest lesson he had ever learned. Five years later that company became the biggest steel corporation in the world (The Bethlehem Steel Company) and Charles Schwab became one of only two people at that time who were paid a salary of £1 million per annum.

The system, like all great ideas, is incredibly simple. You may even be disappointed at its simplicity. But if you are really determined to be a true professional, a star achiever, use this system and it alone will make you as wealthy as you want to be.

Here it is. At the end of each day draw up a list of all the jobs you need to do the following day. Now number them in their order of importance. The following day start at number one on that list and keep at it until it is complete, and then move to the second item and keep at that until it is complete. Then move to the third item, and so on as you work your way through the list. Finally, I must stress that it is crucial that you work this system for at least 30 days consecutively, because by doing that it becomes a habit. Bad habits creep up on us. Good habits have to be developed.

Why did Charles Schwab, who was no fool, pay such a huge sum of money for such a simple idea? Firstly, many people make lists of things to do, but usually they draw up their list first thing in the morning, the most productive time for most of us. They spend their freshest hour trying to decide what to do, instead of utilising that time for *achievement*. So always do it the night before. Secondly, you have to accept that there will be many days when you won't complete the list. But what *has* been done will have been the most important. Thirdly, you should physically cross the items off the list as you complete them. You will subconsciously be more motivated. Seeing ourselves progressing gives us added impetus. The cumulative effect is that every day becomes a day of achievement, not a day of activity.

There is one further tip that is well worth bearing in mind. How do you decide in which order to list your tasks? How do you prioritise your daily activities? This, of course, has to vary according to one's responsibilities in the business. But as a professional salesperson your key tasks must be those that will always get you more sales.

I have always conducted my business activities around these key areas:

SALES            TRAINING            PROBLEMS

Problems are best left until after 5.30, when the majority seem to get solved anyhow! Training, I regard as any process that teaches you or others more about the key tasks.

The professional salesperson should maximise *selling* time. If we look at a salesperson's working day as being total working time (TWT), we should also look at the time he or she spends in contact with clients, customers or prospective customers. Let us call this customer contact time (CCT). Would you agree with me that it is impossible to make a sale unless one is in communication with a customer, either by face-to-face meeting or by speaking on the telephone? We have to be in communication in order to get the YES. If that is so, CCT is of paramount importance to the star professional. Research has shown that, on average, CCT is only 15 per cent of TWT. The professional salesperson has to improve on that.

So where does the rest of the time go? In travelling, report writing, communicating with the office and, perhaps in some rare cases, sleeping in a layby or, on a cold, wet day, tucked up in a cinema — of course not!

But could you find an extra five per cent of your TWT by better planning and organisation, by cutting down on lunch or coffee breaks? This might in your case be just an extra 20 minutes a day, but if that 20 minutes is spent purely in communication with customers or potential customers, theoretically you could increase your sales figures by one third. Theoretically? In *reality* YOU WILL INCREASE THOSE SALES FIGURES.

In training yourself to manage your TWT more effectively, try to avoid wasted conversation and discussion with colleagues. I personally get very frustrated in my own company when I find there is too much talk among ourselves. We only earn money when we are talking to clients.

Try also to handle a piece of paper only *once*. Have you ever noticed how some people handle paperwork? When they open their mail they glance at the letters then sort them into piles. They then reread the letters and put them into further piles: to do today, tomorrow and some other time. In some instances a piece of paper can be handled anything up to twenty times by the same person! What for? Wasted effort leads to procrastination.

You must also be very firm in preventing other people, including customers, from wasting your time. Far too many salespeople allow themselves to waste selling hours waffling with people who give them little or no business but nevertheless tell a good joke or have outside interests in common. Remember, it's *your* bank account that they are pilfering.

Professional salespeople realise that in the management of their time they must allocate time for relaxation, for keeping fit, for their hobbies and families. The enormous demands of this job make it very easy to neglect its purpose which is to provide a better standard of living. So *do* allow time for your families and create events so that they also have something to look forward to.

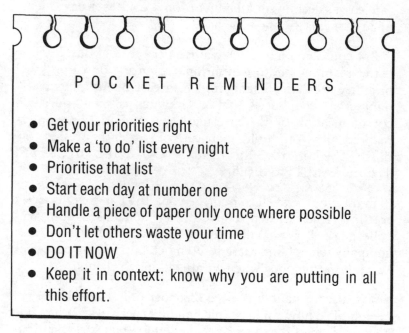

POCKET    REMINDERS

- Get your priorities right
- Make a 'to do' list every night
- Prioritise that list
- Start each day at number one
- Handle a piece of paper only once where possible
- Don't let others waste your time
- DO IT NOW
- Keep it in context: know why you are putting in all this effort.

**‘    WISE    WORDS    ’**

The less one has to do, the less time one finds to do it in.

Lord Chesterfield

# 5

# *Finding the Business*

People in business will lose a percentage of that business however successful they are, however good their service is, and however well the product is positioned. Changes in market trends are the main cause. Products become obsolete, business moves away or ceases trading, buying authorities change.

One of the principles of professional salesmanship is that you as a salesperson should regard yourself as a businessperson *in your own right*. It must be your responsibility to get new business. You cannot merely wait for customer enquiries or leads provided from marketing or advertising. I learned to my cost the risk of being passive, waiting and hoping for prospective customers to call, write or phone in. Now I never base my future on the success or failure of an advertising campaign. I believe it was Henry Ford who once said, 'Fifty per cent of my advertising works; I only wish I know which fifty per cent.' So, I have to find new business myself and my advice to you is that if you want to be a winner you have to have a good system for finding new business. And it must not be dependent upon the activity of somebody else.

◀ *PAST CUSTOMER LIST* ▶

So let's begin with the richest seam of prospective new business that nearly all companies possess — the past customer list.

It is much easier to sell something to somebody you have previously sold to. There is already a relationship which, in turn, means that there is some common ground. Add to that list past enquirers, who may not have been sold to, as well as customers who may have done business with you in the past but who now no longer trade with you, but remember that the people in those companies may have changed.

Having built a really comprehensive list of contacts, addresses and telephone numbers, it should not be necessary to go to the next stage of sourcing business until you have exhausted the immediate potential. The better your initial list the longer you will be able to prospect new business from relatively sympathetic sources.

I have said that the richest seam of new business is to be found in one's customer base. Now the motor industry has to be one of the most competitive with agents continually offering outstandingly good deals to attract new purchasers. I have been purchasing motor vehicles for the last 30 years and have always bought them from a motor agent. A professional salesperson should surely have contacted me about three months after the purchase to make sure that I was satisfied with the vehicle. He or she should have contacted me again one year later to see if all was well or if I was considering making a change. A third contact should have been made 18 months later, and a fourth two years later, as by now it would be almost certain that I would be exchanging my car. Instead, salespeople are intent on making one-off sales rather than building long-term repeat business.

# ◀ NEWSPAPERS ▶

A few years ago, when we were about to launch our first video-based course on professional selling, we needed to increase our customer base dramatically. We arranged to have all the national newspapers, the major local newspapers and the business journals delivered to two homeworkers who searched them for companies that were advertising for salespeople. They then recorded the relevant company names, addresses, telephone numbers, contacts and any further information that the advertisement disclosed such as type of product and area of operation. This information provided us with a vast resource of prospects. With our course on selling we obviously needed to talk to sales managers. It has proved to be an outstandingly successful system.

# ◀ HOME SALES ▶

The rule of thumb in the sourcing of prospects is to make sure that you contact the right person with the right interests. My friend, Bill Jack, tells a story about his mentor sales manager, Joe Ubrich, who sold sewing machines. He was a true professional and he sold his sewing machines to individual householders — what is often termed as 'door-to-door' selling. He developed a very sophisticated system which made him *the* star in his field. Two weeks before moving into a new town he would place an advertisement in the local paper, advertising a second-hand sewing machine with a box number to reply to. On arriving in the town he would go straight to the post office and collect the replies. He then proceeded to call on each of those prospects, armed with the knowledge that every householder he visited had an interest in sewing machines, whereas his rivals would be calling systematically from door to door, in the hope of being able to raise some interest. He appeared to do much less work than his colleagues, but he was certainly working more intelligently.

There are numerous examples of oustanding salespeople working with greater achievement and less activity — for instance, the burglar alarm salesman who reads his local paper to find out where the latest burglaries have been and then systematically calls on all the houses in the immediate neighbourhood, or the fire alarm salesman who reads or hears of a fire, and then does likewise.

## ◀ REFERRALS ▶

The life insurance industry has always encouraged its salespeople to use the most powerful form of lead sourcing in that industry, referral or recommendation. The stars have mastered the art of ensuring that one sale leads to several more, by simply asking the client, 'Have you, Mr Customer, another relative, friend, colleague or business contact whom we may be able to help?'

When you use the referral system don't waste your breath by asking your customer, 'Is there anybody else?' You will get the same reply as the salesman in the retail store who asks, 'Will there be anything else?' NO, thank you. In asking for referrals, be *specific*. Make suggestions that will help your customers to think of others. Don't leave it to them to use their imaginations!

## ◀ FOLLOW YOUR CUSTOMERS ▶

What about those customers who move on to other companies? So often salespeople concentrate on the company and the new person who has replaced the previous contact. Follow your customers and their careers. Remember the old adage: 'Once a customer, always a customer'. *Your customers are people, not companies.*

◀ ## BUSINESS CARDS ▶

Spread your business cards as far and wide as possible. Yes, I agree that this is passive lead generation, and that you shouldn't base your income on the passive approach. But it is very gratifying to get those extra calls and enquiries. Whenever you pay a bill anywhere, leave a business card. Leave your business card everywhere you go.

◀ ## SOURCES OF NEW BUSINESS ▶

1. Past customers
2. Past enquiries
3. 'Used to supply' list
4. 'They said "NO" ' list
5. Contacts that have moved
6. Trade directories
7. Local papers
8. New openings or job enquiries
9. Trade magazines
10. Collecting business cards
11. Referrals and recommendations
12. Other departments within a company
13. Addresses and telephone numbers from delivery vehicles
14. Exchange of information with competitors
15. People moving house.

It is possible to purchase lists of prospects in almost any category that you may require. This is now an extremely sophisticated business and there are numerous list brokers throughout the country that can provide an excellent service.

# ◀ THE PASSIVE APPROACHES ▶

1. Advertising
2. Direct mail
3. Leaflet drops
4. Inserts in journals, newspapers.

## POCKET REMINDERS

- It is essential to get new customers every year
- The richest seam of business is the past customer list
- Use newspapers and journals
- Referrals are cost effective
- Follow your customers.

## ' WISE WORDS '

It is not enough to have a good mind, the main thing is to use it well.

René Descartes

# 6

# *Getting the Appointment*

The vast majority of people involved in our great profession actually loathe making the sales appointment. And in many cases, otherwise professionally able and successful salespeople are pretty useless in using the telephone to fix a sales meeting (presentation). But the true professional must master this part of his or her business. So let's go through the stages that will make it easier. Making it easier will, of course, make the results more effective.

◀ *STAGE I* ▶

This is the process of tuning your prospect list. If there is any uncertainty about who is the buying authority in each case it is now that the telephone call should be made to the prospective company.

Dial the company, and ask the switchboard operator quite

simply, 'Can you help me please? Who is responsible for ...?' Having got the name, do not ask to be connected. If you are asked the purpose of your call say that you want to make sure that your letter is addressed to the right individual. But let me repeat, while you are sourcing information, you have not got yourself into the right frame of mind for the next stage — fixing the appointment.

◀       **STAGE II**       ▶

You must now decide whether to make your first approach by telephone or letter. Neither is more 'correct' because of the variance of industry types, so I will deal with both.

## THE LETTER

Remember that the purpose of writing a letter is to sell your follow-up telephone call which should, in turn, sell the appointment. Another great principle of salesmanship: *you can only sell one thing at a time.*

It is very important that you do not include product brochures, literature or any further information at this stage. Remember, the purpose of the letter is to sell the telephone call, and the telephone call will sell the appointment. It should go without saying that you should not send out more letters than you are able to follow up with the necessary telephone calls.

It would seem appropriate at this stage to mention direct mail as this is becoming increasingly sophisticated and far more common. But I do not intend to go into any detail on how to construct direct mail pieces, and this is best handled by a specialist. The average response to direct mail is between one and two per cent. There are, quite naturally, many specialist direct mail houses which can, and regularly do, increase these percentages, but it is now a finely tuned industry, and should not be approached in an amateur way.

**Figure 7**   A sample introductory letter

6 July 1988

Mr J Smith
Job title
Company name
Address

Dear Mr Smith

May I introduce myself and my company to you.

The purpose of this letter is to inform you that we have one or two new developments within our product/ service/range which may be of great interest to you.

I obviously have no idea at this stage if this is the case, so I will be telephoning you within the next seven days to see if we may be able to fix up a very short meeting where I can explain in more detail our latest product/service/range.

I look forward to speaking to you.

Yours sincerely

Signature
Name (typed)
Job title

## THE TELEPHONE CALL

Firstly, always dial the number yourself. *Never* get a secretary or telephonist to make contact for you. When the switchboard operator answers, ask for your contact by name:
    'Mr Smith, please.'

Don't waste time by cluttering up the process with unnecessary words:

'Would you put me through to Mr Smith please?' You will now be connected to his office or his secretary. If his secretary answers, just repeat your request, but this time use his first name as well:

'John Smith, please.'

She will probably ask who is calling. And your response should be just your name: 'Richard Denny, here.'

Never use a title, such as Mr, Miss or Mrs.

Very few telephonists and receptionists are properly trained in the UK, and I find it an abomination when calling a company to be asked, 'Who's calling?' instead of, 'May I ask your name, please?' and even worse is the request, having given your name, 'From where?' What they mean, of course, is 'From which company?' I have found an excellent antidote. I say, 'From Devizes' (the location of my head office). There is always a deathly hush on the phone at this point. But I get put through very quickly!

If you are asked the name of your company, give it. If you are asked why you are calling say that it is in connection with your letter.

If for any reason your contact is not available, always say that you will call back and ask for the most convenient time. Another great principle of professional selling is that you must never leave the next move to the client or customer. YOU must ALWAYS be in total control.

If your prospect is engaged or busy, do not wait on the line as your enthusiasm will diminish. It is wasted, unproductive time and only makes profits for the telephone company. Always call back.

Now let's proceed to the conversation to secure the appointment.

'Hello, Mr Smith, this is Richard Denny here of Results

Training Limited. Did you get my letter? Good. The purpose of me ringing you is, as I said in my letter, that we have one or two new products/services/ranges that may be of great interest to you. But I really have no idea at this stage so, in order to save a great deal of time now, may I suggest that we fix a short meeting at your convenience? Do you have your diary available? Would 9.20 next Thursday be convenient? Or sometime the following week?'

Let's now analyse this very basic telephone procedure. Bear in mind that you must adapt this outline to suit your own personality and your own industry. Remember too, that you must stick to the principles of *success*.

1. Do not attempt to sell or discuss your products in any detail over the telephone. This book is not about telephone selling because that is also a sophisticated and specialised process in its own right.

   Do not allow yourself to be drawn into a discussion. The purpose of your telephone call is to get the appointment. If your product or service can be sold over the telephone, then get the knowledge and perfect that mode of operation.

2. Do not make a statement that you cannot justify.

3. Do not offer an appointment time on the hour as that may appear to be an appointment that could last an hour, and likewise do not offer on the half hour. Always choose an unusual time because this clearly gives the impression that the meeting will be short. One addition that I personally find useful is to say, 'The meeting will be short, unless you have some points of interest you would like to discuss.'

4. If your prospect says, 'Can't you put something in the post?' the commonsense approach is of course to say, 'That is the purpose of me wishing to see you; so that I can only leave you the information that you will be interested in. Anyhow, Mr Smith, I would really like to meet you.'

◀ *THE COLD TELEPHONE METHOD* ▶

1. Decide before you start how many calls you are going to make and exactly how long you will spend making them.

2. Make sure you have all the information from the prospect list.

3. Follow the above procedure in getting through to your prospect.

4. Make sure that you always make a prime desire statement, that will elicit this subconscious response from the prospect: 'I want to hear what you have to say. I want to see what you have to offer.'

   - We have some new developments that could save your company a great deal of money

   - We have a new product that could make your company a great deal of money

   - We have a new service that could be very cost effective for you

   - We have a new system that could be extremely labour-saving for you

5. Remember the purpose of your call is only to sell and get the appointment.

The script suggested for the primed call can be adapted for the cold call with the following addition. 'Hello, Mr Smith. My name is Richard Denny. My company is ... and we specialise in ... We have a new product/service/development ...'

We use this script in *my* own company, Results Training Limited, for setting up and getting appointments for our Training Consultants to meet with Managing Directors, Sales

Directors, Personnel Directors, Marketing Directors, for our video-based training courses. Our field analysis shows that we have a 90 per cent success rate in making sure our Training Consultants are in front of the decision-maker(s).

You may decide that it is well worthwhile confirming the appointment the day before the meeting is due. You must decide yourself according to your industry type and experience. There are some industries where it is much more professional to follow this procedure, even to the extent of confirming the appointment by letter. Such a letter should always be brief, yet polite (see Figure 8).

**Figure 8**   A sample letter of confirmation

> Dear Mr Jones
>
> It was good to speak to you today.
>
> I am pleased to confirm our meeting/appointment on ... (date) at ... (time) at your office, and I look forward to meeting you.
>
> Yours sincerely
>
> Signature
> Name (typed)
> Job title

Before we leave the important matter of getting appointments I recall a very successful direct mail shot from a client of mine who must remain anonymous. I refer to it as the *page 2 close.*

He sent out what appeared to be only the second page of a two page letter:

..*/2*

As you will see from the above, there will be enormous benefits to you and your company and I look forward to receiving your instructions in due course.

Yours sincerely,

They enjoyed, as you can well imagine, a quite phenomenal response rate!

# ◀ SOME TIPS ON MAKING THE MOST OF ▶ YOUR TELEPHONE CALLS

1. Always smile while you are speaking on the telephone. It does project a better telephone manner.

2. Be enthusiastic. Enthusiasm is very infectious.

3. Stand up from time to time. Have a long lead on your telephone so you can move around. We always sound more decisive when we are on our feet, rather than lounging around.

4. Always plan your call.

5. Know what reaction you want.

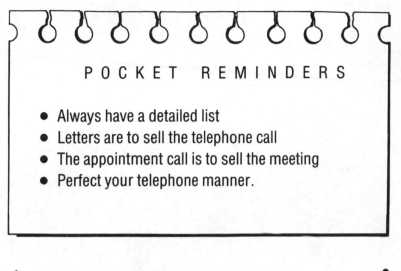

P O C K E T   R E M I N D E R S

- Always have a detailed list
- Letters are to sell the telephone call
- The appointment call is to sell the meeting
- Perfect your telephone manner.

'          W I S E     W O R D S          '

**Practice does not make perfect. Perfect practice makes perfect.**

Vince Lombardi

79

# 7

# *The Rules of Professional Selling*

If you should decide to take up football, the first stage would be to learn the rules. And in learning those rules, you would obviously want to be taught from the current rule book, not from the rule book of the thirties, forties or fifties. Regrettably, too many salespeople are being taught out-of-date sales practices.

As I have already said, the buying public is more sophisticated than it used to be. People are better educated; they have more choice and the competition is more intense and proficient. It is therefore absolutely essential that any salesperson attempting to perform and achieve in the vibrant market-place of the nineties, must be equipped and knowledgeable on the accepted practices of *modern* selling.

In listing these rules I must again stick firmly to the principles, and those principles have to be adapted to the selling environment or industry. In so many cases these rules are commonsense and appear to be stating the obvious. But it is exactly these rules that are being broken by salespeople who fall into the 80 per cent category.

Over the years, in working with client companies and training thousands of salespeople, I have continually heard our 80 per cent category salespeople telling me and showing me by their body language that they have *heard it all before.*

The Star Performers, or as Tom Hopkins, the American sales trainer calls them, the Champions, are hungry and willing to be reminded of those rules and principles because they know that there are few truly new sales techniques that really work. It is the sound principles of people to people communication that are the most effective, and it is these principles that get forgotten and neglected.

## ◄ RULE I  SELL TO PEOPLE ►

Selling is only directed at *people.* You can't make a sale unless it is to another person.

So the rule is: understand that every sales presentation must be different because you will never find two identical people.

Every prospective buyer has different aspirations, requirements, wants and needs. They come from different homes, they work in different business or office environments. They have different pressures to cope with and different targets to achieve. They have different people to report or respond to. They have different family backgrounds, different educations, different hobbies and interests and different goals. They may be happy or unhappy; they may be disillusioned or frustrated; they may be positive or negative. The professional salesperson has to

- *Become a people expert*

  I hate using that word, 'expert'. It has often been defined as a combination of an 'X' (a has been) and a 'spurt' (a drip under pressure). Unfortunately, in this context, you really do have to be an expert, in the best sense of the word.

- *Actually like people*

  Be *interested* in them. You must attract people to yourself. Clients and customers should look forward to their meetings with you or to hearing from you on the telephone. Tom Hopkins describes the Champion as a 'pully person not a pushy person'.

◀  # RULE II   SELL YOURSELF  ▶

Everybody has heard, more than likely at an induction course, that what you have to do is *go out and Sell Yourself*. But very few people are actually taught *how* to sell themselves. We all agree that it is very important, but how is it done?

The answer, of course, is to be interested in other people. Ask questions and get people to talk about themselves. People quite naturally are interested in themselves. In all reality, it is their biggest interest of all! If you don't believe me, imagine a family wedding or a Christmas gathering. All the family is together, somebody produces a camera, and the family group photograph is taken. Two weeks later you get your print. Who do you look for first? Grandma? Auntie Mabel? No, you don't! You look for *you*; and you look terrible!

In getting other people to talk about themselves, notice their environment, pictures on the walls, any indication of hobbies, sports and so on. Now I am *not* suggesting that one should be smarmy, but I am suggesting that people are truly fascinating and that if you approach every meeting thinking, 'I am going to like you, and you are going to like me', the right chemistry can be *engineered*. It is also quite extraordinary how much you can find in common with the most unlikely people. You meet somebody for the first time at a party, and you discover that at one stage you both lived in the same town or even the same street. A bond is created which can develop into a relationship. The simplest things can act as a glue. So do attempt to find some common ground and remember another great principle of selling, *people buy people*. None of us does business with a person we don't like if we have a choice. If there is no choice then of course you have to complete your transaction, but we all prefer to do business with people we like. I am, of course, a buyer as well as a seller, and in my business we buy a great deal of print. We are continually called upon by printers and stationers who want our business, but the vast majority of our purchases are from one printer. He is not always the cheapest, he doesn't always give us the best delivery, but he is a really pleasant chap.

Many years ago, before I started selling as my new career, I was farming. I recall the occasion when a new sales rep called at my farm: 'Mr Denny, my name is Chris Bowles. I represent Silcock Lever Feeds.' He was selling cattle and pig feed and all these brands are very similar. 'I have just taken over this area. I am calling just to introduce myself as I expect you are very busy. I will pop in again in a month's time, if I may.' And with that he left a business card and departed.

One month later there he was again. 'Remember me, Mr Denny? I am Chris Bowles from Silcock's.' We chatted for a few minutes. He asked me how things were going and I told him not very well, because all farmers are trained to say that! He said, 'I won't hold you up. I will see you next month.'

The following month I greeted him with 'Hello, Chris.' I told him that one of my calves wasn't doing very well. He suggested that a bag of his calf food might help so I bought one. Within a couple of months, Chris Bowles was supplying me with *all* my feed requirements. I did not purchase Silcock Lever Feeds, I purchased Chris Bowles.

So, sell yourself. Be interested in people and find the common ground.

◀   ## *RULE III   ASK QUESTIONS*   ▶

If you were to ask me what I consider to be the single most important skill in mastering the art of professional selling, I would say it is the ability to ask questions.

Just prior to moving our offices from London to Devizes in Wiltshire, we decided we needed a telephone answering machine. I arranged for three companies to send their salespeople to make their presentations.

Number one arrived with his answering machine in one hand and his briefcase in the other. He came into my office and proceeded to demonstrate his answerphone, telling me what it would do and how it worked. He then attempted to close the sale. I got rid of him.

Number two used an almost identical technique. He made a thorough demonstration, explained the guarantee and took me through the user's manual. He also attempted to close the sale. I got rid of him.

Number three arrived and he didn't appear to have anything. He chatted for a few minutes and then said, 'Mr Denny, in order to save a great deal of time, may I ask you a few questions about your business and your requirements,' to which I obviously replied, YES. He then asked me why I wanted a telephone answering machine. Guess what I said?!

He asked me how many incoming calls we expected each

day. He was very *interested* in our business; he asked me if we wanted a facility to take messages off the telephone away from the office, he made notes of my replies and after some time, he said, 'Well, I think I've got just what you are looking for.' He went out to his car and brought in a telephone answering machine (I bet it was the only one he had). He told me what his machine could do, in the context of what I was looking for, and you can guess who got the sale! He had the courtesy and the *professionalism*, to discover my exact requirements.

In asking the right sort of questions remember the principle of 'Selling to Win' — you can only sell to people and no two people are identical.

Remember that the interests of a managing director may be very different from those of a sales director, a personnel manager, a production manager, a housewife, or a professional buyer.

A managing director in most cases will be primarily interested in his or her company profits. A sales director, on the other hand, will be primarily interested in sales. A professional buyer will want to get the best possible value and delivery time, whereas a personnel manager is primarily concerned with the interests of staff. As there are so many variables you must prepare your own list of questions according to your industry and, of course, to the people that you will be selling to. So build your own checklist.

If you are going to be a true professional, never attempt to sell without preparing these questions in detail. This, in itself, requires planning and thought. Ask the right sort of questions, ask questions that lead towards your unique selling points, to a positive response. Ask questions that will give you a YES response. Use your questions to discover your prospect's prime desire. Find out as much information as you can about budgets, how much they are expecting to pay, how much money they have. So many salespeople are *afraid* of talking money until the end of the presentation. And, finally, always have a pad of paper to write down the answers and make notes. If you are in a meeting with another professional, a doctor, for example, or a solicitor, wouldn't you be surprised if they didn't make notes?

# ◄ *RULE IV   LISTEN* ►

Now this is, of course, common sense. But sadly very few salespeople really listen. They *think* they are listening but what they are really doing is thinking about what they are going to say next. Most of us have two ears and one mouth, and that's the ratio to keep in mind when you're using them! Listen to what is said, as well as listening to what is not said.

The salesperson who masters the art of asking the right questions, and of listening carefully to what the prospect has said, will find that most customers give numerous buying signals.

An enquiry about price is a buying signal; an enquiry about a delivery date is a buying signal; an enquiry about colour or style is a buying signal. Listen out for the problems or worries which your client may have. A professional salesperson realises that he or she is a *problem solver*. Nearly every sale solves a problem.

# ◄ *RULE V   LINK FEATURES TO* ► *BENEFITS*

There is, of course, a very clear distinction between the features of a product or service and the benefits of that product or service. In reality, the customer is interested in purchasing the benefits only. It is the benefits that they want not the features.

Let's take the example of a motor car. The features of this model could be that it has power steering, electric windows, automatic door locking, overdrive and a sun roof. Now let's link those features to the benefits. This vehicle has power steering which means that it is light to handle, particularly in small areas, and after a long journey you will certainly arrive feeling less tired. It has electric windows which means that from the driver's seat you can easily adjust any window, so stopping the frustration of having to lean across and wind down a window. It has automatic door locking which means that when you shut and lock the driver's door, all the doors are locked — particularly useful on cold, wet days. It has overdrive which means that you will have greater fuel economy and with the price of petrol, this could be a well worthwhile saving. And it has a sun roof, which is an excellent feature for those gloriously hot, sunny days, when you can press a button, slide back the roof and have the sun streaming in.

You will notice I have used the link phrase WHICH MEANS THAT. Don't over use this phrase, but it is a very useful reminder not to over sell *features*. There is also a very useful test that you can apply, not only to yourself but to any salesperson you encounter who seems only to be selling the features. This is the SO WHAT test.

The salesperson says that this car has overdrive — SO WHAT. The salesperson says his company is the market leader — SO WHAT. We are the biggest ..., largest ..., smallest ..., longest established ..., nationwide ..., local ... All of these are SO WHAT features. What really matters is what it means to the buyer . 'We are the largest' means, 'We have the experience and resources to satisfy your requirements'. Many salespeople become so obsessed by their own company and products that they fail to realise the importance of relating such statements to their customer's benefits.

Before we leave the subject of features and benefits, it is imperative to remember that the true professional talks only about the features and benefits that relate to their customers, and that every customer is different. For example, the car salesman who strongly sells the features and benefits of the cocktail cabinet installed in the motor car, but who doesn't take the trouble to find out if his prospect is a teetotaller, could lose the sale, or at least bore the customer while he labours the feature.

## ◀ *RULE VI    SELL THE RESULTS* ▶

Don't sell your products or services. Sell the *results*, or what your product or service will do.

A customer who walks into a hardware store and asks for a quarter-inch drill doesn't really want one. What the customer wants, of course, is, a quarter-inch *hole*. He can't buy that so he states his requirement as being a quarter-inch drill.

Within my group of companies we have a small publishing company and its leading title is an outstanding reference book called *The World Travel Guide*. For some years this had been available only to the travel industry and had very much become the travel trade's bible. I realised that this book would be excellent for business and more general commercial use. We decided to increase its circulation rapidly. Selling it to individual businesses is, of course, very easy, but we wanted to create some big volume sales. It occurred to us that the banks could be a very useful customer.

So we researched the benefits and presented them to a major international bank. We pointed out to our first prospective client that, by providing their foreign till branches with *The World Travel Guide*, the cashiers would become more knowledgeable, more aware and better able to give a really good service. We pointed out that customer queries on information could be sourced immediately, and that the foreign till clerks would be more interested in their work because they could relate currency transactions to the destinations of their customers. We pointed out that the clerks and cashiers would be able to provide useful information about early closing dates, for instance, and public holidays.

Furthermore, we offered to each of the bank's branches some tips on how best to use the guide to give better customer service. That sale concluded with an order of one thousand copies. Two things stand out:

- We discovered the prime desire of our client — better customer service, as all the banks are working in a very competitive environment
- They could see clearly the benefits to them and how they could use those benefits

That sale started with a completely cold approach.

I have said earlier that the professional salesperson does not *have* to be a great talker. He does not *have* to have the 'gift of the gab' but he must be able, when necessary, to be enthusiastic about his product or service and he must be able, through what I can best describe as 'picture power', to convey the benefits and results to the client. Picture power uses words to describe, to create pictures in the minds of the listeners. Facts or features do not create picture power images. Descriptive phraseology most certainly won't. Enthusiasm will.

# ◄ RULE VII  DON'T RELY ON LOGIC ►

What is it that causes people to make a decision to buy? Is it logic or emotion?

The Harvard Business School did some research on this some time ago and they discovered that 84 per cent of all decisions are based upon emotion and not logic. I have said that people buy people. I have also said that we will not do business with somebody that we do not like. These are, of course, emotional reasons. Too much poor selling is based upon purely logical selling.

In the out-of-date sales rule book, salespeople were trained to find a need, to prove a need and to sell the need. All this does is create hard selling techniques. And again, as I have already said, hard selling is out of date.

I could prove to you very quickly that you NEED some more life insurance. Or, if you haven't got any, I could prove that you need some right now. But let me ask you a question, 'Do you *want* some?'

The good and professional life insurance salesperson will find the need but he will not *sell* the need. He will turn that need into a WANT, by selling the results of either having or not having. The professional life insurance seller is able to tell countless horrific stories of people who have had insufficient or no insurance, and the sadness and traumas created for their families. Good selling turns that emotional appeal to the advantage of the seller, and creates a want.

The true professional believes in his or her product and does everything possible to persuade the client to insure according to status, income and the desire to provide for the client's family.

So what are the chief buying emotions?

- Health
- Security
- Prestige
- Fear of loss
- Pride of ownership
- Ego
- Ambition
- Status
- Greed

This is another great principle of professional selling. People will always find the money for the things they want, not necessarily for what they need. Where you are 'need selling' your prospective customer will be much more concerned about price. If you are selling screws, say, to a professional buyer and his task is to buy screws in order to complete a manufacturing job that his company have been commissioned to undertake, it will be harder to stimulate an emotional want. He has been told to purchase screws and his job is to buy as well as possible. He will, of course, be buying value, but nevertheless he needs those screws so he is obviously going to be much more price conscious.

Some readers of this book may have been brainwashed and conditioned by the importance of finding the NEED and selling it. In this more competitive world, where salespeople have to be professionals in order to win, it is vital that you don't sell the need. You must still *find* the needs, but turn those needs into a want by the use of negative or positive picture power. Sell the end results.

# ◀ RULE VIII BE SELECTIVE IN THE ▶ USE OF PRODUCT KNOWLEDGE

Product knowledge is for the benefit of the seller not the customer. It is very rare that the person who knows most about the products is also the best person to sell them. In depth product knowledge is essential for professional salespeople, not only for their own belief in what they are doing but, more importantly, for their own self-confidence and credibility. I find it dreadfully frustrating to talk to uninformed salespeople. But the reverse is equally frustrating: sellers who are so in love with their product that they give every detail of its history, production and technical specifications. They get some of the best educated prospects, but very few customers! Remember — people don't buy products they want the *results.*

A short time ago, I was commissioned by one of the UK's largest building societies to train its managers to sell mortgages. In my brief, they explained that building society managers over the years had been brought up in a very different economic climate, one in which customers would have to put their name on a waiting list and *apply* for a mortgage. Now, with greater competition and vast sums of money available, mortgages have to be *sold*. Would I teach their managers how to sell mortgages?

'No,' I replied, I wouldn't do that. 'But that's what we want,' I was told, 'We must sell more mortgages.' 'No,' I insisted 'Your customers don't want a mortgage!' They *say* that they want a mortgage; they *ask* for a mortgage; but what they *want*, of course, is a home. As soon as they get a mortgage, they will want to get rid of it. I don't know anybody who loves their mortgage. What we've got to do, is to train your managers to sell the results and the fact that your society can provide the best possible service.'

Quite naturally they agreed with the principle and I was commissioned to implement the training programme.

# ◀ RULE IX    IDENTIFY YOUR UNIQUE ▶
## SALES POINTS

This rule will help you to beat the competition in the most competitive sales environments.

Every business, every product or service, has something that is *unique*, and you as the professional must take time out to be sure in your mind exactly what your USPs are. Knowing what they are and knowing how to use them will certainly help you to win business when you are up against tough competition.

Let's take the motor industry once again as an example.

Competing motor agents, selling identical vehicles or models, far too often reduce their prospects of profits by ending up in a price war. The salesmanship of uniqueness is based upon a cheap price. They may not have unique points about the vehicle but their USPs may be their service, their after-care attention, their methods of part-exchange, the siting of their premises, or even their sales professionalism, their interest in the client.

In being able to find out whether the USP will be of interest to the prospective customer, how can you use them to beat the competition? Go back to the asking stage, to rule III. Ask questions that lead your prospect towards your unique sales points.

'Would it be important, Mr Prospect, for you to deal with somebody who gives excellent part-exchange value?'

'Would it be important, Mr Prospect, that the agent you purchase your vehicle from can provide full, after-care service?'

'Would it be important for you to make your purchase and then deal with one person who will be always available to deal with any problems that may arise in the future?'

Would it be important for you to deal with an agent that is close to your home for easy access?'

These are questions which lead towards USPs. If the answer is YES, record on your note pad. But do not *sell*. As we will see when we come to the full sales presentation there is a time to research, to ask for and to assimilate information and there is a time to sell. Take the time to create your USP: it will put you clear of your competitors.

In some very competitive industries, business is gained by tendering. Tender documents are prepared, submitted to applicants and decisions taken by faceless committees that the salesperson can very rarely present to. So they are unable to use their professional salesmanship in acquiring the business. But many specifiers, before preparing the tender, will arrange meetings with interested parties, gain information and find out what is available. The professional salesperson will, at that meeting, go through the process of turning their USP into a need and then into a want. Your USPs can then often be built into the tender document. Once again, you have removed the competition. No professional salesperson will go out into the market-place without absolute confidence that *he or she can beat the competition* because there is always something different, something unique to offer.

**Figure 9** Identifying your own unique selling points

Identify your own unique sales points in the three key areas.

1  Product or service    _____
                         _____
                         _____

2  My company            _____
                         _____
                         _____

3  Myself                _____
                         _____
                         _____

# ◀ RULE X    DON'T CATCH 'PRICEITIS' ▶

'Priceitis' is the disease caught by the 80 per cent category. They feel, think and then believe absolutely that in order to make a sale they have to be the cheapest. These 80 per centers are convinced that customers buy the *price*, that they buy only the cheapest.

I recall the first sale I ever made. I was farming at that time and desperately needed to supplement my income with some further business activity.

I travelled to London with six very large, free-range eggs, which in those days the packing stations would not take. I had previously arranged an appointment to meet the buyer of a well known grocer in Knightsbridge, called Harrods. My first presentation consisted of offering these six eggs in a nice box, with some straw. I explained to the buyer that these eggs were brown. He could actually see that and when I paused for breath, he quite naturally asked me the price of my eggs. At that time, large eggs were retailing at 3s 6d a dozen. When he asked me the price I said, 'My eggs to you, Mr Bowen, will be 7s a dozen.' Silence. I shifted from one leg to the other. And when he said, 'I'll take 300 dozen to start with this week.' Now, at that time I actually didn't have any eggs to sell! I was involved in dairy and pig farming, but there was a lot of profit and I was able to purchase eggs from my poultry-keeping friends to satisfy the order. I then went on to build a very successful wholesale and retail business on the back of that very first order.

But let's look at the *principle*. My eggs were unique at that time because they were free-range. Secondly, they were a little big larger. Thirdly, I was so inexperienced a salesman that I didn't know any better! It had never occurred to me that people might buy the price.

There are very few products that are truly price-sensitive and, as we have already seen, the more the product is purely a need, the more price-sensitive it is.

A few years ago in the UK, the market for petrol was extremely price-sensitive. Price changes were normally announced at midday on the television and radio. As soon as a price rise was announced (they never went down) people would leap into their cars, head for the nearest filling station and then sit in a queue for two or three miles, possibly with a few empty cans in the boot, in order to save just a few pence and beat the price rise.

Nowadays, petrol can fluctuate from station to station by as much as 10 pence per gallon, and there don't appear to be any queues outside the cheaper ones!

If it were true that people buy *only* the price, the cheapest motor car in Britain would be the biggest seller, and we all know that this is not the case.

On my training courses I continually hear the 80 per cent category bemoaning the fact that their products are too expensive *only* if they were a little cheaper, they could sell that much more. *If only* these same salespeople would realise that cheapness does not mean security. I personally would much prefer to work for a company that is making realistic profit margins for my future.

Anyhow, if customers buy only the price, there is no need to employ salespeople at all. All that is necessary is to send out the price list and the brochures, and wait for the orders to come in.

Let's be absolutely certain of this great principle: *People Buy Value*, or their perception of value, not price. So professional salespeople sell value and not price. Don't ever be afraid of, or embarrassed by your prices. Be proud and be positive because any fear will be conveyed instantly to the customer. If you subconsciously think that you are too dear, if you think you might lose out because of your price, your manner, your body language and your lack of enthusiasm will betray you.

Don't ever apologise for your prices. Your product knowledge and the service that you offer demonstrate that your prices are fair.

# ◀ *RULE XI   DON'T JUST TALK, SHOW* ▶

It has been said that people buy more with their eyes than their ears.

Now, as with every rule of selling, this can be taken too far. I hired a new sales manager when we launched a new video course, a distance learning course on the management of people with full support of books, trainer's guides, examination papers and certificates. The sales manager's first task was to employ a team of five field sales consultants and their job was to call on prospective purchasers having had an appointment already set with the buying authority. After two months of activity, and poor sales figures, I went out into the field myself to see what was going on. And here was my new sales team, from one of the most respected training organisations in the world, making the most classic of all presentation mistakes! They were walking into clients' offices armed with the video course in the belief that good products sell themselves. They were sitting down in front of clients and immediately saying, 'Well, I expect you want to see the videos.' They then spent anything up to one hour showing the client the video.

They were selling products, not results, and our sales results were disastrous.

We naturally retrained. Then we remotivated. Then we achieved outstanding sales figures.

But it is a rule of selling that you must *show*. As we saw with rule III, however, the product demonstration should relate to information; the benefits can then be shown to their best effect. Don't present or demonstrate your product until you are ready, until you have the right information.

Many of you work in an industry in which it is impractical or downright impossible to show your products. You may be equipped with a presentation file of photographs, or armed with slides, or a portable video unit. But do remember that these are only an aid for your sales presentation, *they will not do the job*. Many salespeople in that 80 per cent category bemoan the fact that they don't have sufficient product brochures. They spread them like confetti. They devalue the content with their excessive distribution.

Product brochures are again an aid, they will not necessarily make the sale. And if the product brochures are so good that they do the job, again, who needs salespeople?

One further tip: whenever you are presenting or demonstrating any product, your hand movements affect its value. Be it a brochure, a piece of equipment, or the product itself, may I suggest that everything that you handle, whether it belongs to you or your company, should be handled as if you are handling a piece of antique porcelain — with feeling, with respect and with utmost care.

◀ ## RULE XII   DON'T KNOCK THE COMPETITION ▶

This should be commonsense. There is very little to add to this rule. But it is equally important that you don't *fear* the competition. We have talked about the fear the 80 per cent category have for competitors' prices, but one principle of professional selling is that if you are not concerned your client won't be. And the reverse is just as true. If you show concern about the competition, your client will be concerned as well, will lose confidence in you and will want to research what you have to offer in more depth.

In my business I am continually asked about other training companies. 'Very good operation; quite good training', or 'Been in business for years; little bit old fashioned nowadays, but very nice people'. I smile and show a sense of humour and that helps to develop a comfortable relationship. I personally have no fear about competition anywhere in the world. And I don't believe my sales team has either.

In some sales situations your presentation will be just one of many that your client has organised. They are looking to see what is on offer and you will be proposing against a competitor. Don't fear it. Ask, in the politest way possible, about other companies your client may be seeing and then using your industry knowledge, steal the thunder from your competition. Explain your competitors' USPs, because they will if you won't. Then, when your competitor labours his or her own USPs, it will all appear to be a little 'old hat' and you will have stolen their thunder.

Another tip: in this selling environment, always try to get yourself into the position of going in again at the end of the meeting schedule.

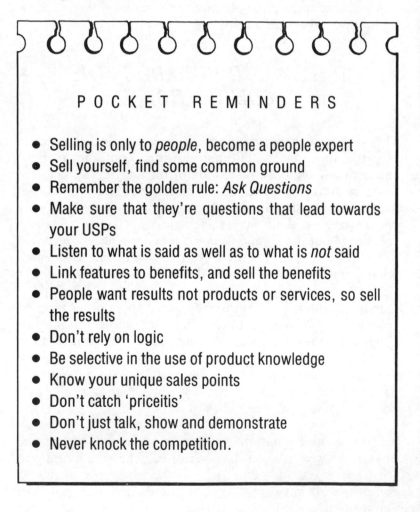

## POCKET REMINDERS

- Selling is only to *people*, become a people expert
- Sell yourself, find some common ground
- Remember the golden rule: *Ask Questions*
- Make sure that they're questions that lead towards your USPs
- Listen to what is said as well as to what is *not* said
- Link features to benefits, and sell the benefits
- People want results not products or services, so sell the results
- Don't rely on logic
- Be selective in the use of product knowledge
- Know your unique sales points
- Don't catch 'priceitis'
- Don't just talk, show and demonstrate
- Never knock the competition.

**'** WISE WORDS **'**

Salesmen are the very lifeblood of industry. They are said to be born, not made. Nothing could be further from the truth. Intelligent individuals can be trained. It is time that salesmen acquired proper status and had their importance to industry correctly assessed.

Sunday Times, 8 September 1985

# 8

# *The Sales Presentation*

You may recall that I said that if you are going to play a game which you have never played before, the first stage is to learn the rules, and that you will, quite naturally, want to learn from the up-to-date rule book. You will, no doubt, play as close to those rules as you can without breaking them or without being caught. But the true professional plans each game according to the strengths and weaknesses of the competition. In other words the tactics for each game will be preplanned.

I am, of course, using this as a metaphor for selling.

You are now armed with the rules. Break them, and you will suffer the consequences. Now you must plan each presentation.

I am now going to take you through the pure, unadulterated theory of a classical sales presentation. You don't have to run through all seven stages of the sales

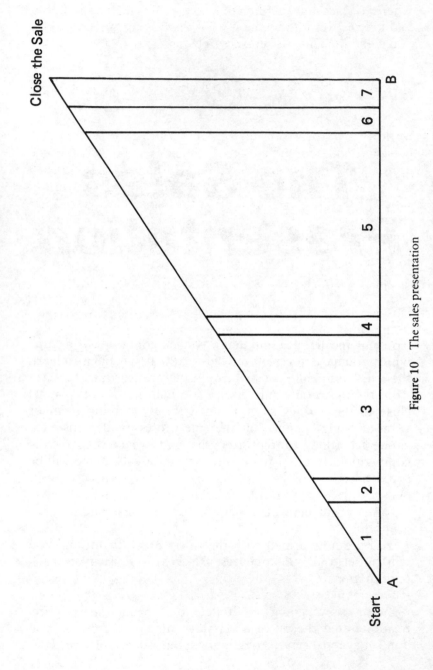

Figure 10   The sales presentation

presentation every single time. Your experience will tell you where to start and the direction to go. But unless you know and keep within the boundaries of the classical presentation, you will diminish your chances of being the true star.

# ◀ *THE SEVEN 'CLASSICAL' STAGES* ▶

So now let's proceed through the seven stages of the classical presentation. Look at Figure 10. Point A is the start of the presentation and we are going to take our client to point B of the presentation, which is, of course, the agreement to conclude the business. Notice that the process is divided into seven segments. These indicate the approximate length of time to spend on each segment.

## STAGE 1 GETTING YOURSELF ACCEPTED

This is the time spent establishing some common ground, finding out about your contact, getting to know your prospect, and selling yourself. Don't overdo this. Don't waste people's time. Read your prospect's body language, and assess the type of person that you are dealing with.

## STAGE 2 THE OPENING PRIME DESIRE STATEMENT

You must say something to elicit a positive response (even if it is subconscious) from your client. Get him or her to think, 'I want to hear what you have to say.' Let me give you an example:

> 'Mr Prospect, we have some policies that *could* increase the security of your operation dramatically, but I have no idea at this stage, so I need to find out a little bit more about you.'

Remember the principle: *never make a statement that you*

*cannot substantiate.* So, in the example I have just given, I have made an opening prime desire statement, but I have qualified it to reduce any chance of causing offence.

> 'Mr Prospect, we have a training course that I *believe* will almost certainly increase your sales; but may I ask you a few questions first before telling you about it in detail?'

> 'Mr Prospect, we have some new products that would probably get you more business, a stronger customer base, and be altogether very profitable for you. But may I ask you a few questions first of all?'

You must also keep in mind the greatest selling principle of all: *we sell to people and everyone is different.* An opening prime desire statement has to be tailored according to the person you are selling to, because they don't all have the same wants or needs.

## STAGE 3 ASK THE QUESTIONS

As figure 10 shows, this is a major part of the presentation. So ask the questions, make some notes, *don't* provide any solutions, and most of all *don't do any selling.* Ask until you are absolutely certain and remember that your questions should lead your prospect towards your unique selling points. And questions which demand YES as answers create a good buying environment.

## STAGE 4 CHECK AND PRE-CLOSE

This is the professional really at work — making sure you have got all the relevant information, making sure you are now playing by the buyer's rule book, making sure you know what parameters the buyer is operating within. Check as follows:

> 'Mr Prospect, is there anything else that we have not discussed that you may be looking for?'

or,

> 'Mr Prospect, have I got all the information, or is there anything else we have not discussed?'

In other words, find out if you now have got the information, the buyer's problem, in order to proceed to offer the solution. If your client says YES, or is in any way encouraging, go to the next stage of professional selling. Find out how serious your prospective customer really is, because we all know some prospects can be great time-wasters. So now pre-close your sale along the following lines:

> 'Mr Prospect, if our product or our service will do all the things we have just discussed, will you be placing the business with me? ... Now I am not, Mr Prospect, saying it *will*, or that I *can* provide the service. What I am asking is if I can match up to what you are looking for, will you give me the order?'

If at this stage your prospect says YES, proceed with the presentation, and you have pre-closed your sale. If at this stage your prospect says NO, or refuses to commit himself, don't go any further yet. Say:

> 'If that is so, Mr Prospect, there must be something else that we haven't yet discussed.'

He may say, 'I want to see the competition', or 'I want to discuss this with someone else', or 'the price has got to be right'. All these are *buying signals*. All are points of specification to now add to your list. Write them down and let your prospect see you writing them down. And now go back to stage 4 again.

> 'Is there anything else, Mr Prospect?'

If he says no, proceed once again to the pre-close.

> 'Mr Prospect, if I can satisfy you on all of these points,

including those I have just written down, will you place the
business with me?'

If he says YES, proceed to the next stage. If he says NO, you
could be confronted by a wally. Either he doesn't know what
he wants or he is in no position to make a decision. He is
wasting *your* time, time you could possibly be spending
elsewhere making sales. Your experience will, of course,
determine your next move.

I must emphasise this — *you are a professional seller.*
Don't let the wallies waste your time! Far better to leave
politely with the doors open.

## STAGE 5 THE MARRIAGE

Now at this stage, and only at this stage, should you start to
sell. Sell your products, their features, the benefits to the
customer and then, of course, the *results.* Only at this stage
will you be able to provide the solutions. At stage 1, of
course, you are quite naturally selling yourself. But from
there to stage 5, no selling whatsoever should have taken
place. Now, remember and put into practice all the rules of
professional selling. Link the features to the benefits. Sell the
results. Sell your unique selling points. And, above all, sell
only the benefits that relate to your clients' requirements or
interests. Don't tell them about features they won't be
interested in, and don't oversell. And at this stage of your
presentation, if you are given any buying signal whatsoever,
or if your client indicates a willingness to proceed, *do not go
on selling.* Stop your presentation and complete your
paperwork or agreement forms. Our 80 per cent category
lose many sales by overselling. They talk their customer out
of a sale!

The marriage, as we have called this stage, is the point at
which you match your client's wants with your product or
service. Do this well and the sale is automatic.

## STAGE 6 THE FINAL CHECK

Ask your client a gentle question: 'Mr Prospect, how does that sound from what I have explained to you?' Or, 'Mr Prospect, are you satisfied with what we have discussed?' Or, 'Mr Prospect, we seem to have covered all the points. Is there anything else we haven't looked at?'

You see, while you were going through the marriage, you should have ticked those points that you listed as being important to your client. Your prospect will have seen those items being physically ticked off and, no doubt you will have got agreement at each stage of the discussion. So the check is there to make sure that he or she is comfortable. If you have confirmation at this stage, proceed to stage 7. If your client or prospect raises objections at this stage, it will be either because you did not ask the right questions during stage 3 or because you have not convinced him of the benefits during the marriage. In which case, you may have to backtrack to find out the point at which you have not been sufficiently convincing.

Many salespeople in our 80 per cent category like to introduce the price at the end of a presentation. I suppose that the reason is their fear of the price, fear that it will lose them the sale. If the price is going to lose them the sale it will lose it for them at the beginning, and I cannot see any point whatsoever in going through all the work of a sales presentation just to be defeated by a price objection at the end. That has got to be downright crass *stupidity*. I have never met one buyer who is not deeply interested in the price. I don't know anybody who walks into a shop and does not look for a price tag. This does not mean that they are buying the price, but of course people are interested in price, and price should be discussed at the questioning stage, then justified and then value built in at the marriage.

## STAGE 7 THE CLOSE

This is too important to be a section. We need a whole chapter to discuss closing the sale.

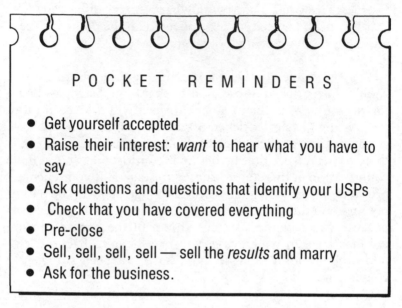

### POCKET REMINDERS

- Get yourself accepted
- Raise their interest: *want* to hear what you have to say
- Ask questions and questions that identify your USPs
- Check that you have covered everything
- Pre-close
- Sell, sell, sell, sell — sell the *results* and marry
- Ask for the business.

**      '        W I S E    W O R D S        '**

**Luck is what happens when preparation meets opportunity.**

Bits & Pieces

# *9*

# *Closing the Sale*

There is far too much nonsense written, spoken and taught about *closing the sale*.

Closing techniques have an aura of mystery. Many salespeople become conditioned by the closing mythology. They believe that if they are armed with sufficient closing techniques they will become stars. The very word 'closing', in itself, has become a death trap for unsophisticated and unprofessional sellers.

The closing of the sale is not some special technique that is suddenly unleashed at the end of a presentation to persuade the unsuspecting to buy. The master professional knows that the close begins in the first seconds of the meeting. And there is a clear distinction between closing a sale and helping a procrastinator to make a decision.

By now you will have gathered that this book is about *professional* selling. I am laying out clearly all of the stages that are necessary to master the art and be a winner. So I am not suggesting new, *untried* techniques that *may* cause a prospective purchaser to submit and make a decision to buy without realising what he or she is doing.

Sales training has been living in a gimmicky world for far too long. Too many salespeople have been let loose on the buying public with an amazing closing technique which gets people to buy what they don't really want. It isn't difficult, as I have said before, to get people to buy things that they don't really want. But all that does is to cause problems later — lapsed policies, cancelled sales, noisy and embarrassing complaints. But at the other end of the scale I detest weak selling, and salespeople who don't close the sale. It is far better to get NOs than a jam-packed pipeline full of MAY BEs.

Let's now discuss and, I hope, dispel some of the misconceptions about closing sales. It has been said that the salesperson should close early and often. Of course that is right. When the customer is ready to proceed, gives buying signals and indicates that he or she is now satisfied, the sale should be closed. So complete the necessary paperwork. And often? Yes, of course, I agree with that. Why accept just one NO as the answer? Some of my own most successful sales have begun with, 'NO, I am not interested', or 'No I don't think that's right for us', or 'I'm completely satisfied with what I've got now'. Star salespeople throughout the world say that they get, on average, five or six NOs before they get the YES. It comes back to attitude and to determination to ask for the business. Persist, and find out how best to convince the prospect. Keep in mind the basic principle, *people like buying*. They don't necessarily like being sold to, but they *do* like buying.

There are numerous closing techniques. The majority have been dreamt up not by star salespeople but by trainers. They liven up their sales courses with what may appear to be the ultimate technique but, in reality, they are untried and unused. They are unworkable in the real world, with real people who aren't as stupid as the trainer makes them out to be. You could use the Half Nelson or the Full Nelson, the Puppy Dog Close or the Sharp Angle Close, or even the Last Ditch Close. One day I hope to meet a wealthy salesperson who remembers the 100 techniques for closing. I meet many very poor salespeople who can recite them verbatim!

Closing 'helps people make decisions that are good for them'. You must help the prospect to make up his or her mind, and the hard truth about selling is that it is about *closing* sales. You can't make a sale without closing because *selling is not order taking*. The foundation of sales training has been built upon the mnemonic, AIDA:

- Attention
- Interest
- Desire
- Action.

'Action' is, of course, closing the sale.

# ◀ *THE GOLDEN RULE OF CLOSING THE* ▶ *SALE*

Once you have asked any form of closing question to conclude your business discussions, SHUT UP.

There is not a star salesperson in the world who will disagree with this. The 80 per centers, when they *do* actually get around to asking for the business, all too often start talking again.

I remember explaining this technique to my eldest son, Lyster, when he was sixteen years of age. He had advertised, in our local paper, a music centre that he wished to sell. When the first person arrived he made his presentation and he showed how the equipment worked. The prospect then, quite naturally, asked the price (the greatest buying signal of all). Lyster gave the price. Then he shut up. The prospect stood on one leg and then on the other. He lifted the lid, and put it back down again. He turned the knobs, looked round the back and underneath and neither said a word for at least two minutes, which seemed like three hours to Lyster. Finally the customer said, 'I'll take it.'

Many sellers can't bear what they perceive as the pressure of the silence even though the only person suffering the pressure is the seller. It is quite uncanny — the longer the silence, the more certain the reply is to be YES.

You see, closing the sale starts right at the very beginning, with those first few words at that first all-important meeting.

Closing the sale is *not* what the salesperson does after the presentation. It is *not* just a question of putting together a sequence of words to corner the prospect. Closing the sale is the *whole* of the process. It is the presentation, the communication, the seller/prospect empathy: it is following all the basic rules.

We saw in the last chapter the basic structure of the sales presentation. Now, obviously, a salesperson in a retail outlet, say, is not necessarily going to follow all those stages. A salesperson calling on a prospective buyer in a busy store will not necessarily pull out a pad of paper and go into a detailed needs analysis or research, for instance. But the principles are the same, even though they can be adapted or adjusted.

Closing the sale, however, is a must in *all* selling environments. So how should the professional ask for the business?

It should, *of course*, be automatic if the classic presentation has been followed. Having checked that the prospect is happy with what has been offered, one of the three closes can be used.

1. 'Fine, let's complete the paperwork.'

2. The choice close:

> 'Do you prefer to pay by cheque or cash?'
> 'Do you want red or green?'
> 'Do you want twelve or thirteen?'

3. The minor point close:

> 'Will you be requiring ten extra handbooks to go with your course, or twelve?'
> 'Do you want metallic paint on the car?'
> 'Would you like a set of shoe trees to go with your shoes?'

Very simple and basic common sense. Isn't it extraordinary how effective the simple systems can be? You see, if you keep to the rules of selling the close becomes entirely automatic. You don't need some strong arm method to corner your prospect into submission. They *want* to proceed; they are *looking forward* to taking delivery or commencement of the service; they are *relieved* that their problem has been solved; they are *delighted* that at long last a salesperson has had the courtesy and professionalism to do the job correctly.

◀ **DIFFICULT CLOSES** ▶

Some prospects just can't or won't make a decision. Some will procrastinate. Others hope the decision will be made by somebody else. Others actually *fear* making buying decisions. So let's now look at one or two ideas for handling people in those situations. Remember the words of Heinz Goldman, one of the all-time greats of sales training: 'The star salesman does what the others don't do.'

## THE BUCK PASSER

Firstly, you must be absolutely sure that this character does have the authority to make the decision. You should establish this clearly at the questioning stage of the presentation, by asking: 'Would there be anybody else, Mr Prospect, who might be involved in making the decision to purchase, own or invest?'

If you establish that the prospect does not have the authority to make the decision, it is necessary to close him from the point of view that he really does want what you are selling: 'Just supposing that your board of directors likes what I am offering, will you agree that we should proceed?' Or, 'Just supposing, Mr Prospect, that they say YES, will you agree to that decision?'

If your prospect now replies in the affirmative, you should then make your presentation to those who have the authority to make the decision. I always say something along these lines: 'Fine, Mr Prospect. Well it's obviously in both our interests for me to meet them as I am sure that you would not want anybody else presenting *your* product or service for you. And anyhow, they may have worries or questions that only I could answer. So let's fix a meeting right now, and save a lot of your time.' Or, 'Mr Prospect, it would seem sensible for me to meet up with your Mr Jones and discuss our products with him as well. This will save a lot of your time. I can also answer any questions that he may have, and I'll be only too pleased to do it for you. Let's fix up the time now and make a firm appointment.'

## THE PROCRASTINATOR

This is the prospect who just can't make up his or her mind. They really want it, they know it's right, you have satisfied all their worries but you are still unable to close the sale. Try this: 'Mr Prospect, from everything that we have discussed, you know it's right. If you make the decision I will give you the security and total protection of your investment. Let me give you a written undertaking. Firstly, if the price goes up during the next thirty days, you will still be able to purchase at the old price. Secondly, if the price goes *down* during the next thirty days, you will have it at the lower price. Thirdly, you will have the right to cancel at any time during the next four days.'

## THE DEFERRED DECISION

This is the prospect who says, 'We will be making the decision in a week's ... a month's ... six months' time. Try this: 'Mr Prospect, may I ask you what your decision will be dependent upon?' Now, obviously, what you say next depends on your prospect's reply. But let's suppose he says, 'We have discussed your proposal, and we will be making the decision at our next management meeting. There is no further information we require, as you have already provided that to everybody concerned.' Take out your diary and ask your prospect, 'Exactly what day is your meeting? What time would you like to see me on that day, or the day after?'

And then make sure that your prospect makes a note of your next meeting in his diary.

### DO YOU HAVE IT IN BLUE?

This is where the prospect, once you have gone through the whole presentation, raises a previously undiscussed query: 'Do you have it in blue?'

The professional salesman, if he knows he has got it in blue, will say, 'Let's make a note of that,' and will immediately write it out on his order form. If you are uncertain about your ability to supply to the new specification say, 'If I can supply it in blue, will you go ahead?' The danger here is that you are, of course, deferring the decision.

You will have gathered that the whole purpose of closing the sale is to tie down, to make decisions and be completely in control of the next stage.

## THE FOR AND AGAINST CHART

In a really desperate situation with a prospect that you have been unable to close, in some instances it may be worth clearly identifying for your prospect the FORs and AGAINSTs. This should be done with integrity and professionalism, bearing in mind that it is the duty of the professional salesperson to help customers make up their minds. So on a sheet of paper, clearly draw up a list of what is for and what is against. This often helps them make a decision.

Professional salesmanship is the *solving of problems*. But you must close the sale, and get decisions to proceed made. Do always remember that when your prospect has made the decision it nearly always comes as a great relief.

◀  # NOT CLOSING  ▶

During the sales presentation, at stage 4, we have the check and the pre-close, at which, having asked all the right questions, you should know how you intend to conclude the sale. If at the pre-close stage your prospect will not agree to proceed, it is at this stage that you should leave. Having been so derogatory about some salespeople, we should also be realistic about some prospects. There are time wasters, and there are some wallies! Don't waste your time selling to them, but always leave with a polite parting and the door open. For example, 'Well, Mr Prospect, it seems absolutely pointless me wasting your time, and in this instance even more importantly, mine, by telling you about our products if you won't proceed. So if, and when you are ready to discuss them, here is my business card and my telephone number, please give me a call. I'll call you again in about a year to see if your requirements or circumstance have changed.'

It is immensely satisfying for salespeople occasionally to walk out on a prospect. It's very good for one's ego!

One final reminder: do be aware of the weak seller's trap. If your prospect says, 'It all sounds very interesting, but I'll tell you what to do, leave me a brochure', you can be pretty sure that the only person who will profit from that arrangement is your printer. Sales brochures are an aid to selling. The vast majority, when they leave your offices, are stored in waste paper baskets or forgotten files. In many cases the request for a brochure is the prospect's polite way of saying, NO.

So whenever you are requested to leave a brochure only do so on the basis of having fixed your next meeting. Make sure that you are in control of the next stage. Leaving brochures only leads to procrastination on both sides. I am horrified by the number of salespeople who peddle sales literature. It's all activity but no *achievement*, and as far as my own sales executives are concerned, they are forbidden to write on their activity reports, 'Left a brochure.'

There is a saying that goes, 'A stranger is a friend I have not yet met.' I have found, over years of selling, that the vast majority of people that I have sold to also become friends. I am pleased to meet them again and I believe they are also pleased to meet me.

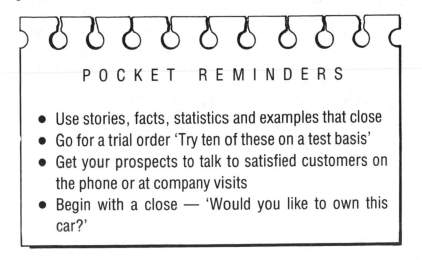

POCKET     REMINDERS

- Use stories, facts, statistics and examples that close
- Go for a trial order 'Try ten of these on a test basis'
- Get your prospects to talk to satisfied customers on the phone or at company visits
- Begin with a close — 'Would you like to own this car?'

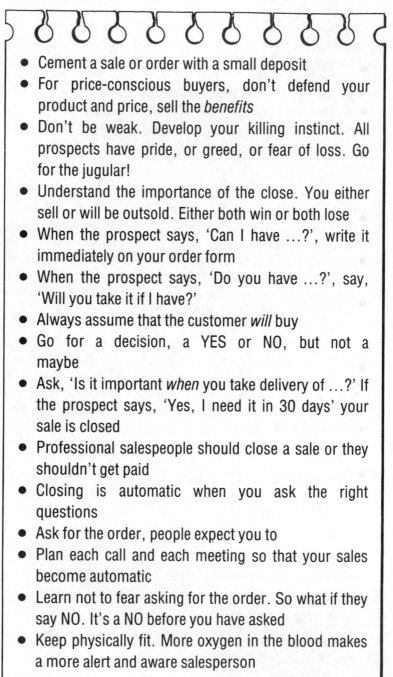

- Cement a sale or order with a small deposit
- For price-conscious buyers, don't defend your product and price, sell the *benefits*
- Don't be weak. Develop your killing instinct. All prospects have pride, or greed, or fear of loss. Go for the jugular!
- Understand the importance of the close. You either sell or will be outsold. Either both win or both lose
- When the prospect says, 'Can I have …?', write it immediately on your order form
- When the prospect says, 'Do you have …?', say, 'Will you take it if I have?'
- Always assume that the customer *will* buy
- Go for a decision, a YES or NO, but not a maybe
- Ask, 'Is it important *when* you take delivery of …?' If the prospect says, 'Yes, I need it in 30 days' your sale is closed
- Professional salespeople should close a sale or they shouldn't get paid
- Closing is automatic when you ask the right questions
- Ask for the order, people expect you to
- Plan each call and each meeting so that your sales become automatic
- Learn not to fear asking for the order. So what if they say NO. It's a NO before you have asked
- Keep physically fit. More oxygen in the blood makes a more alert and aware salesperson

- Be a good news carrier. Always have some good news for your prospect
- Sell with *enthusiasm*, it is infectious and irresistible
- Continually review your sales performance
- Mentally debrief after each presentation — the good, the bad and the ugly. How could you have done it better?
- Outstanding service alone can become your greatest closing tool
- Don't ignore other people — wives, husbands, secretaries, assistants, juniors
- Don't have pound signs in your eyes — you will never be a professional salesperson while adding up your commission
- Remember, *emotion* sells, not necessarily logic. Tell stories of either success or failure that relate to your client and are examples of your product or service. Stories are very persuasive and close sales, but they must be true
- You are in the *people* business, so every meeting, every presentation and every conversation will be different. Don't learn some of the above phrases like a parrot. Your communication must reflect your personality and beliefs.

**'** WISE WORDS **'**

One of life's little ironies is that when you finally master a tough job, you make it look easy.

Richard Denny

# 10

# The Principles of Professionalism

This chapter considers the points of detail that can make a great deal of difference to your performance. They are the success ingredients of the star professional.

Imagine a horse race in which the finish is so close that only a photograph can distinguish the winner. Winning 'by a short head' can mean the difference between a prize of £25,000 and a prize of £5,000. Did the winning horse have to go five times faster in order to win five times the amount of money? Would the jockey have gone through five times more training in order to win? Did the horse perhaps consume five times the amount of oats? Of course not. The jockey and the horse did just a little bit more, and maybe that little bit more came in the last furlong. So many salespeople fail to put the extra effort into the final furlong or, worse still, they are not even aware of the professionalism they need to apply in that final furlong to make them a great winner. And I believe that salespeople should look at themselves as winners or losers.

So let's now run through some qualities that winning professionals have in common.

◄      **MAKE IT EASY TO SAY YES**      ►

A few months ago, I had to attend a convention in Atlanta in the United States. I telephoned an hotel that had been recommended to me. The receptionist on hearing that I was telephoning from England, asked if I was attending this particular convention. He then asked which flight I was coming in on, and what type of room I required. He told me that he had a room available, and quoted a price. Finally he said he could arrange for a car to collect me from the airport and take me straight to the hotel. It made it very easy for me to say YES. He sold me the room, and I was left with a very warm feeling. I had been dealing with a real professional and I was looking forward to enjoying what I had just bought.

Do make it easy for your customers to say, YES. If you have a lot of paperwork to complete, make it easy for your prospects. Don't give them all the forms to take away and fill in. I have bought vast amounts of insurance over the years and I am always thrilled to find a salesperson who will help me to fill those forms in easily. Nowadays I flatly refuse to do business with any broker who expects me to understand the jargon and terminology of their trade.

Don't complicate the decision-making process.

◄      **BOTH WIN OR BOTH LOSE**      ►

This is a great principle of selling. The salesperson must believe that selling is not a situation where he or she wins and the customer loses. When a sale is transacted, both should be winners. And if the sale is not transacted, both should be losers. This is an attitude of mind that develops among star professionals because they believe totally in their products.

They will only sell to a prospect if they believe that it is right for their prospect and that their prospect will be a winner having made a purchase.

If you believe that your customers are going to be better off having done business with you, then that alone will increase immeasurably your communication skills, your confidence, and your credibility with your client or prospect.

◄ ## *DON'T PREJUDGE* ►

We all know the importance of the first impression. When you meet people for the first time you instinctively form an opinion of them in your own mind. It happens all too often that a salesperson prejudges a prospect, and either rules out the possibility of making a sale too early, or grossly exaggerates the potential business. Salespeople in the 80 per cent category all too often underrate or overrate the potential of a prospect.

◄ ## *DON'T CATCH BIG CASEITIS* ►

This is a complaint often caught by salespeople who have permanent £ or $ signs in their eyes. You know the sort — the ones who chase money rather than sales. They are *always* going for THE BIG SALE.

They spend so much time trying to catch the big one that they miss out on the millions of small sales that can provide a substantial income. Many sales trainers will say that a big sale is just as easy to get as a small sale. In principle this is true. The method is the same. One does not need extra skills in order to close a bigger case. The principles and the professionalism and the rules are all the same. But there are obviously fewer big sales to win so the rewards for getting them are naturally higher. The professional will, of course, be working to win some big ones. But when they come, they must be regarded as the icing on the cake. Don't allow yourself ever to be trapped into just going after the big one.

◀  **REPLACE THAT SALE**  ▶

I have for years now worked on the assumption that *every* presentation I make will automatically result in business. But the purpose of the presentation is to replace that sale with another. It does not occur to me that I am not going to close the sale. Each sale is one for the benefit of the customer the minute I have a chance for a meeting. But what I am going for is a recommendation or a referral to a new contact, or a new department or additional sales in the months or years to come. Selling, as we have said repeatedly, is a business.

It is, as usual, all a question of an *attitude*. In Chapter 3, we discussed this vital factor, the one that makes the star stand out from the crowd, that puts them in the 20 per cent category. A positive attitude manifests itself in all forms of action or communication.

So how does one replace the sale? Realistically, of course, one must first complete the initial sale, but while I am in discussion I am constantly listening for further opportunities, and I will actively suggest to my client that they recommend my services to others. I actively seek names, contacts and telephone numbers from them, and in some circumstances ask them to make a phone call there and then for the introduction.

If you seek to replace one sale with another, your presentations will be that much more concise, helpful and positive.

◀ ## WATERPROOF THE SALE ▶

In some industries, it is necessary to understand the buyer's emotional response to the purchasing decision. Many people suffer from what I can best describe as 'buyer's remorse'. They have decided to purchase, they place the order or even make the payment. But within a few hours, they question themselves. No doubt you must have done this yourself. Maybe you have bought a suit or a new dress and as you walk away from the shop you glance at other shop windows to see if you could have bought better. You might even show somebody else when you get home, in the hope that they will encourage you. You might walk past a shop window and you see the same item offered at a cheaper price. All buyers have these feelings at some stage, so it is very important to understand how people will feel when you have made the sale. They will often discuss their purchase with others, hoping for reassurance, but we all know that the world is sadly lacking in positive, constructive people offering positive, constructive advice. They are much more likely to cast doubt, they are much more likely to condemn or destroy if given the chance, much more likely to pull down that buying decision.

Some customers will question their decision even without the help of others. They get cold feet, and wish to cancel the sale. So the professional, being a master of people-to-people feelings, will understand this reaction when it occurs in his own industry. The professional counters this buyer response by waterproofing the sale.

How? Very simply and easily. Having concluded the transaction, say to your client, 'I will call you tomorrow to discuss any worries you may have, because overnight you may have thought of something that we haven't already discussed. And it is far better to discuss those worries with me than with somebody else because I can get you the information.'

In some instances it may be necessary to make a follow-up visit. But whatever you do, don't allow sales to be lost because of your unwillingness to follow-up.

I know of some very successful salespeople who, once they have transacted a sale, ask their customer to make a list of any concerns they may have. These professionals then contact their customer within 24 hours to discuss those points.

I was taught some time ago that the sale is not complete until the goods are giving satisfaction. (Another way of putting it is, as my own financial controller says today, that the sale is not complete until we get paid for it!)

◀     *PLAN EACH CONTACT*     ▶

In our earlier chapters on finding the business, getting appointments, and organising one's time, we discussed the importance of planning each stage. The professional salesperson sets a goal with each action. Your very first meeting with a client might have the objective of only establishing a relationship. The objective may, on the other hand, be to get a sale there and then. The variance, of course, depends upon your circumstances.

Never attend a meeting with the attitude of mind, 'Well, I'll see what happens'. You will end up by wasting your own time as well as your prospects. If you have made a presentation and your client delays making a decision for whatever reason you will, of course, be compelled to make some follow-up telephone calls. *Plan those calls.* Have a clear objective in mind for each one, even to the extent of planning a little bit of good news to pass on. Plan a *reason* for that call. Think of further points that you could make to prod your prospect into a buying decision. And remember always the principle of professionalism we discussed earlier: make it easy for them to say YES. I get very frustrated with the 80 per cent category contacting me just to see how I am. They aren't interested in how I am at all! They are just *hoping* that I will give them a decision. They don't offer me anything else to help me to make it. But let's be clear about what I am saying here. I am *not* saying that you should offer a discount, or an amazingly better deal in order to conclude the business transaction. Although there are obviously some cases when a better package presented to a prospect can quite naturally sway the decision-making process in your favour (which, in turn, will be to their benefit).

The true professional does *nothing* without a plan, an objective, a goal. And the true professional will always have another move up his sleeve.

◀ ***VARY YOUR VOICE*** ▶

Some people, without realising it, speak in a monotone and their otherwise very interesting thoughts can become extremely boring. They speak at one speed and they speak at one pitch.

May I suggest that you carry a pocket tape recorder once or twice, and record yourself in conversation. Hearing oneself is normally a pretty unpleasant experience but it is worth trying to establish whether or not you are interesting to listen to. Enthusiasm, of course, dramatically increases one's chance of being interesting from a listener's point of view. It is always much more comfortable for listeners to be confronted by an enthusiast. If you have something very important to say pause before you say it, and then pause again afterwards.

As we found when we considered the close, there is tremendous power in silence.

◀ # BE TRUSTWORTHY ▶

I am not saying this because you aren't! But *in the minds of your customer* trust and reliability are paramount. Customers, like everyone else, prefer to deal with reliable people so always *do what you say you will do*. If you are going to put something in the post, *do it*. If you promise delivery at a specific time, *make sure it happens*. Don't make promises that you cannot keep; don't make exaggerated claims that aren't true.

◀ # TELL THE BAD NEWS ▶

This, of course, follows on directly from being reliable. If, for whatever reason, a promise or a guarantee to a client becomes impossible to fulfil let your customer know immediately. Don't let the time when they were expecting whatever it was you promised pass without your being in contact. People nearly always accept bad news graciously, but they very rarely accept discourtesy, downright lousy service and the unprofessionalism of someone who doesn't take the trouble to let them know that they can't do what they had said they were going to do.

◀ # WELCOME COMPLAINTS ▶

One of two things is happening when people claim that they never get a complaint. Either they don't do very much business, or they tell lies about other things as well. If you are doing a lot of business, mistakes will occur from time to time. Now as a salesperson you often have to bear the customer's wrath but it is *far* better they tell you than that they just cease trading with you and tell everybody apart from you why. The average Brit doesn't like complaining. In France, of course, it is the national pastime but here we are easily embarrassed to complain to the *culprits*. But we *do* whinge endlessly to everyone else! Imagine going to a restaurant and having a lousy meal — do you complain? Not until the following day when *everybody* is told, friends, relations, the postman ... *Don't eat there*!

So welcome complaints. Always give a complaint priority. Handle it immediately, listen to what your customer is saying, understand why they are saying it, put yourself in their shoes, ask them what they would like done about it and do your best to do just that. But above all, give any complaint absolute priority and let your customer know that you are giving it absolute priority. No doubt you will already have found that handling a complaint well can turn a one-off customer into a customer for life.

◀          ## SELL OTHERS IN          ▶

Have you ever experienced the service engineer who calls at your home to repair one of your home appliances or maybe the installation engineer who comes to install a new washing machine. Isn't it quite extraordinary how many of them will rubbish the salesperson who sold you the machine? ... or inform you that it is not a particularly reliable model as they are forever being called out to repair this type? The professional salesperson, on the other hand, will always have good words to say about his or her colleagues, support staff, accounts and administration departments. If you are going to suggest that another member of your company should visit your client, sell that person as being a person with ability, with knowledge and experience that will *help your client*. You will do yourself more good by selling other people than you ever will by attempting to be clever and condemning them.

◀          ## BUYER MOTIVATORS          ▶

There are two extremely important buying motivators that professional salespeople must remember at all times:

- The fear of loss
- The opportunity for gain .

And of the two, the fear of loss has to be the greatest motivator. People will fight harder and react more strongly out of fear of losing out than they will for either a personal or a business gain.

How much time would you spend looking for a £10 note you have mislaid? Will you put the same effort into trying to gain a further £10? No. The same applies to business. People react more quickly and respond more positively if they see a possibility of losing out. Some of the best examples of this principle being put to use successfully are to be found in the retail sector. The finest example of all is the one-day sale. I recall a furniture store in Darlington that offered a six-hour sale. It was advertised widely on local radio and in local papers and was a most resounding success. By giving a definite close-off time and being prepared to adhere to it, this store capitalised on people's desire not to lose out on a great bargain.

We have said elsewhere that a salesperson is a 'mind-maker-upper' and by creating a definite time factor you will immeasurably increase your chances of closing the sale. Fear of loss focuses the buyer's mind quite strikingly!

Far too many weak salespeople allow their prospects to procrastinate, to put off the decision to another day, to 'think about it' when in reality they will be doing no such thing. Far too many of the 80 per cent are *put off* by the prospect who 'wants to discuss it with somebody else', a husband, wife, business partner or manager, when, in reality, they can't make up their mind. By imposing a cut-off time, *you cause the decision to be made.*

Let me list a few examples that you may be able to adapt to your own business. (Bear in mind though that the best approach, as always, will depend upon you brainstorming the solution that is most suitable for your own clients and products or services.)

- We must have your instructions within 24 hours or else you will lose out on this quarter's production schedule
- I can guarantee this price and delivery for 48 hours only
- I have advance notification of a price rise so it makes good sense to get the order in now.

In my own business where we are selling my time for client companies we make it absolutely clear that if they are interested in a date for me to speak at a conference or convention, we will only hold that date for 24 hours, after which, if they have not reached a decision, they will lose out. When our sales executives are selling our distance learning courses, they offer the purchaser the opportunity to attend our *Train the Trainer Day* at a special rate if they make a purchase. But as the numbers are strictly limited on these courses, they must come to a decision very quickly in order to guarantee their place.

So whether you are a solicitor, say, selling your time or a specialist salesperson, make sure that you have good and realistic reasons for your customers to make up their minds.

◀ ## *USE THEIR NAMES* ▶

To most people the sweetest sound is that of their own name. But do use it correctly.

In the UK it is still not acceptable for a salesperson to use a prospect's, or a customer's first name until they are invited to do so. In the United States it is perfectly acceptable to use their first name from the outset. Custom varies around the world. Be particularly careful when using the telephone. But do always invite your customers to use your own first name.

Try also to remember the names of people in your business environment other than those with whom you may be doing business. Some misguided salespeople think that their buying authority is the only important person. You should also consider secretaries, receptionists, engineers, technicians — there is an endless list of people — if you want to retain your instructions. All too often a customer with whom you have spent time building a relationship moves elsewhere and an assistant takes over. If you have not developed a relationship and taken the trouble to acknowledge or greet the person, he or she may cultivate a relationship with your competitor.

So do remember that *everybody matters*. You are in the *people business*. Don't forget it.

◀　　　　## SAY 'THANK YOU'　　　　▶

Have you ever thought about sending a thankyou card or even a very short letter to thank a customer who has placed business with you? You can create a great deal of good will by doing this. It takes only a few minutes to put one in the post.

◀　　　## SELL THE 'ADD ONS'　　　▶

I have already said that you can only ever sell one thing at a time. But, while keeping that principle firmly in mind, don't be ashamed to sell the numerous 'add ons' you have.

I personally adopt the attitude that my customers are all dumb. I don't say this with any disrespect whatsoever, but I don't expect them to know all about my business, products or possibilities. They aren't *stupid*, but unless I tell them about everything I can do for them, how can they be expected to know? Their job is to be an expert in their own business, not in mine, and not in what I have available for them.

The professional salesperson will present a prospect with as many possibilities for using their products as possible. So once you have closed the sale, now is the time to suggest the 'add ons'. *Never* say, 'Will there be anything else?' That is a piece of classic naivety. All it will elicit is the quite natural response, NO. By asking 'Will there be anything else?' we are expecting the prospect to know what else is on offer.

When I was selling eggs I used to offer (once I had gained the egg order) cartons for them to be packaged in, 'How many cartons will you require?' When I was selling detergents (once I had taken the order) I always suggested that my customer try out a new product and took a sample order. When I was selling bras on a party plan basis, once I had fitted the customer I would always then suggest a fitting for a mother, a daughter or a grandmother, and fixed a specific appointment. Today, when we sell our distance learning courses, having closed the sale we ask our client how many extra handbooks or manuals they would like to have.

So, always make a suggestion and offer your 'add ons'. You will be surprised at the degree of success it brings.

◀ *GOOD WORDS* ▶

Build up your own vocabulary of good, selling words. And get rid of those which give negative feelings.

| Don't say 'change' | Say | IMPROVE or DEVELOP |
|---|---|---|
| Don't say 'pay' | Say | OWN or INVEST |
| Don't say 'sign' | Say | AGREE or AUTHORISE |
| Don't say 'when I sell' | Say | WHEN YOU OWN |

When it comes to quantity, don't say 'How many are you thinking of?' Say, 'Will ten be sufficient?' If your client says, 'No, no. That's too many. I'll only take five', you are selling well. But whatever you do, *never underestimate. Think big. Get your customer to think big.* This will, of course, also help your negotiating skills because some customers think that by giving you an order for just one, they are a big deal, and may even be looking for a discount on that one. If you are thinking big your customer will be far less likely to ask for a special deal. Equally, it makes it much easier for you to negotiate a special deal if your customer *is* prepared to go for the big volume.

If you think big, you will gradually educate your customers to think big as well.

◀ ## DON'T TALK DOWN ▶

If you talk down to your prospects they are likely to be hostile or defensive. Comments like, 'Well, I expect you didn't realise ...' or 'You probably don't know this', whether true or not, imply that you have more knowledge and experience than they have. You should develop good communication skills by saying, 'Well I expect you *do* know', or, 'I'm sure you are aware'. It is always far better to build people up than to put them down.

Selling *is* communication. It is creating an environment of mutual respect and confidence which is conducive to business. So it is unnecessary, too, to find fault with your customers' previous purchases. All too often our clients know that they have previously made a bad purchase or decision. It serves no purpose whatever to rub salt into that wound. By finding fault you only cause them to want to justify their own or even their colleagues' decisions.

Remember that the seller should be a good *listener*.

◀ ## BE REMEMBERED ▶

Develop your own unique style. Do something that will always be remembered and associated only with you. It may be your enthusiasm. It may be your style of business card. It may be a catch-phrase. But do avoid becoming obnoxious. I know of one particular salesman who, when he shakes hands, intentionally uses such a strong grip that it becomes a bone cruncher. And as he does it he looks intensely into the eyes of the receiver. OK, we all know that a handshake is important, and a firm handshake is certainly better than a wet rag. But like anything else, you can carry your uniqueness of style too far!

◀ **DON'T SIT IN RECEPTIONS** ▶

This may sound a little unusual as reception chairs are obviously put there for people to sit on. But you are a professional salesperson. You are properly prepared and highly motivated, and you will find that on sitting down in a reception area much of your dynamism will end up on the floor. Reception chairs, I have noticed over the years, nearly always seem to be very low. One appears to be at a disadvantage. One also appears to be rather insignificant when someone else comes into or even walks through a reception area. And many people actually look down their noses at somebody sitting waiting for their meeting. You are *immediately* at a disadvantage if your customer or prospect actually comes to get you and you have to climb out of one of these low chairs to shake hands. So *always stand* in a reception area and politely decline offers or even instructions to take a seat. I promise you, you will always feel that much more in command, more confident when you go into your meeting.

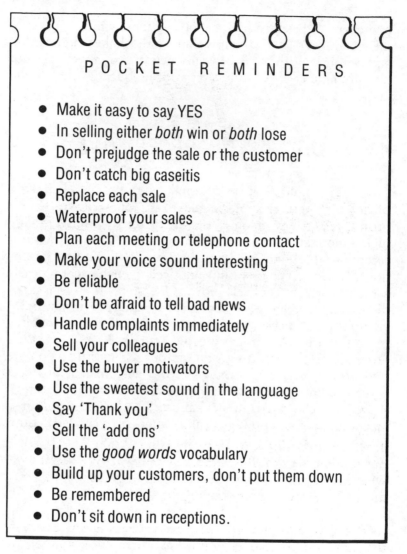

POCKET REMINDERS

- Make it easy to say YES
- In selling either *both* win or *both* lose
- Don't prejudge the sale or the customer
- Don't catch big caseitis
- Replace each sale
- Waterproof your sales
- Plan each meeting or telephone contact
- Make your voice sound interesting
- Be reliable
- Don't be afraid to tell bad news
- Handle complaints immediately
- Sell your colleagues
- Use the buyer motivators
- Use the sweetest sound in the language
- Say 'Thank you'
- Sell the 'add ons'
- Use the *good words* vocabulary
- Build up your customers, don't put them down
- Be remembered
- Don't sit down in receptions.

**' WISE WORDS '**

Experience is the hardest kind of teacher. It gives you the test first and the lesson afterwards.

Richard Denny

# *11*

# *Giving Real Service*

I truly believe that over the next few years, in this rapidly changing market-place, one of the surest and finest ways for anybody in business to beat the competition is to give an outstanding service. But sadly, few people really understand what service is. For salespeople to become successful, they must look for ways of improving the service.

If you were to pick up *The Yellow Pages* of any area and telephone the companies in it asking them, 'Can you tell me please what sort of service your company provides?' I expect that each one will say that it gives a very good service. Now let me ask you as a customer, how many times do you get a really good service, and when was the last occasion you could honestly say that the service you received was superb? You see, *good* service is very rare. Everybody *thinks* they give it but we as customers have great difficulty in *finding* it. So something is going wrong.

# ◀ *THE UNEXPECTED OR THE EXTRA* ▶
## *SERVICE*

Let's return to the example of the motor car. Imagine your car goes in for a 'service'. When you go to collect it, everything on the service checklist has been carried out absolutely correctly. The car is ready on time and the bill is also totally correct. Apart from being pleasantly surprised, you might be forgiven for saying, 'My goodness me, that garage does give a good service.' But it doesn't. What the staff have done is what you are paying them to do — they are carrying out their *trade* correctly.

But if, on the other hand, when you collect your car, you find that not only has the service been done properly, the bill is correct and the car is ready for you, but that perhaps it has also been washed, the interior has been vacuumed, and there is a clean, white sheet of paper in the foot well, you may be impressed. And if there is a band of paper round the steering wheel that says, 'This car has been serviced by Fred Jones. If you have any worries please ask to speak to him,' you would now be inclined to say that the garage has provided a *good* service.

You see, giving a good service is providing the unexpected or the extra — the few add-ons that in most cases cost so little. It is caring for one's customers and treating others as you yourself would like to be treated. Build up your own list of those things that you can do to give your customer a better service. One of the great laws of success states, 'What you hand out in life you will automatically get back.' There is also the law of ten-fold return: 'What you hand out you will get back ten-times over.' The laws of success do not state when you will receive whatever it is you are due! But the certainty is that you will. I pointed out earlier in the book that it is the points of detail that make the difference between the winner and the 'also ran'.

On my first trip to America, I went into an ice-cream

parlour and was confronted with forty different choices of ice-cream. It took me twenty minutes to make up my mind. I had never seen anything like it before. Having made the selection and paid my money the assistant said, 'Thank you, sir, do come again.' I nearly dropped my ice-cream through shock and surprise. In England if I had spent twenty minutes trying to make up my mind which ice-cream to have I would probably have been given my ice-cream upside-down and banned from the shop for life!

## ◀ RECOGNISING CLIENTS' ▶
## ACHIEVEMENTS

Some months ago, I noticed in one of the business magazines, that one of my clients, Simon Davis, had received a major award in the catering industry. I dropped him a short note congratulating him and his company on their achievement. He told me at a later date that it was the only letter he had received congratulating them on their award. I might add that the note strengthened our business relationship and we have since worked together on numerous occasions. So my suggestion to you is, read your trade magazines and your customers' trade magazines and whenever you hear of your clients or customers achieving, winning, or receiving accolades or recognition, drop them a short note (don't include your latest product brochure). Try and send out two or three letters every week to people that you know and can recognise. Now obviously it's not a good idea to write to people that you don't know.

## ◀ HELPING YOUR CLIENTS ▶

Look for ways that you can help your customers to do better. It might be by introductions, by passing on tips that you have heard from another source. Care about your customers and they, in turn, will value and respect your input. There might come a time when you don't have the best possible deal to offer. It is more likely that their buying decision will not be based just on that deal, but that they will value, as I am sure you will, the service that is provided.

◀ **BE POSITIVE** ▶

It is very important to tell people what you can do and try not to tell what you can't. Have you ever telephoned a company and asked them to send you an engineer as you have a problem at home? Isn't it extraordinary how often you will be told that they can't send somebody out to you for two days. Or that they can't do it just at the moment. We always seem to get told what the company, organisation or utility *can't* do. They very rarely say what they *can do*. And what do we in turn feel, or indeed, say? — what a lousy service! Of course, what they should say is something like, 'Thank you for telephoning. I'll have an engineer with you in two days', or 'We will get somebody out to you on Thursday'. Whenever a person says what they can't do, they are sublimely indicating that they are not doing their job properly. So, if your customer asks you to arrange delivery for tomorrow don't reply, 'No, we can't do that'; always counter with a positive response.

◀ **THE PERSONAL APPROACH** ▶

Some research was once carried out in a department store to test the quality of service that customers were receiving. Part of the research was an experiment. On one group of counters, when the assistants gave the change and the receipt to the customers, they put it directly into their hands and some physical contact was made. On another group of counters the change was either put down on the counter to be picked up, or it was actually dropped into the customers' hands. The customers were then monitored as they left the store. It was discovered that the customers who had had the change put into their hands thought the service was very good, whereas those who didn't, said the service was poor.

Now, I am not suggesting that as professional salespeople you have to go around 'touching up' your customers, but what I am highlighting is how customers perceive good and bad service.

In the retail trade, and I include any service from behind the counter such as banking and the building society industry, the first and most important stage of giving good service is the welcoming smile of the person behind the counter. Then, quite natually, the next stage is to use that person's name.

◀ **HANDLING YOUR PRODUCT** ▶

If you ever have to demonstrate your product or handle anything that belongs to you or your company, and I include here price lists and product brochures, it is imperative that the hand movements should be as though you are handling a piece of rare porcelain. If you treat anything belonging to you as though it is priceless, your customers will value it as such. And when we, in turn, hand over something in that manner, again we are providing a much better service.

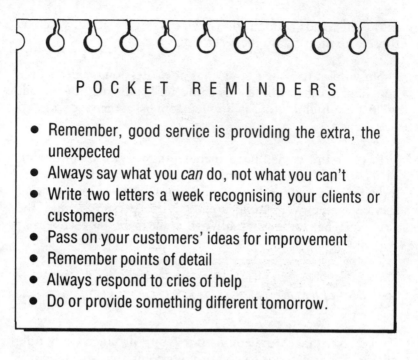

POCKET  REMINDERS

- Remember, good service is providing the extra, the unexpected
- Always say what you *can* do, not what you can't
- Write two letters a week recognising your clients or customers
- Pass on your customers' ideas for improvement
- Remember points of detail
- Always respond to cries of help
- Do or provide something different tomorrow.

' WISE  WORDS '

**A lie may take care of the present, but it has no future.**

Richard Denny

# *12*

# **Handling Objections**

Far too many sales trainers over-emphasise the importance of handling objections. Too many books on selling give the objections handling sequence, and preferred solutions, disproportionate importance in the overall sales process.

When a prospective customer raises an objection it is because he or she has not been convinced. The customer is uncertain or has worries that have not been satisfied. In other words, the customer has not been sold to properly.

◀ ## *PREVENTION NOT CURE* ▶

I truly believe that people *like* buying but they like being sold to well. Customers find it distasteful to be sold to unprofessionally, so the real emphasis concerning objection handling should be on prevention rather than on cure. It is no more than common sense to prevent objections arising rather than to solve those that do.

Let's just recall one of the great principles of selling: both win *or* both lose. If we follow that concept selling is not a boxing match in which the customer throws a punch with an objection and the seller counters with an answer, which provokes the customer to throw another and so on. Poor selling raises objections, and if you find you are getting a lot of objections, the first place to start looking for remedies is with your presentation.

Most products or services contain one or two objections that will regularly crop up. The professional salesperson will have firstly the confidence and secondly the knowledge (as well as the belief in the solution) to counter those objections during the sales presentation. In other words, the objections should be pre-handled at the selling stage of the presentation. Find out if those objections are pertinent to your particular prospect during stage 3 of the presentation, the questioning stage. You will then know if you are going to have to pre-handle the usual objections.

Let's look at some examples with this in mind. Suppose that you ask your prospect at the questioning stage, 'How important is the price to you, or are you looking for value?' If the prospect replies, 'Well, I have already had a price in from Fishman Contractors. Let's see what you come up with,' and you know that Fishman Contractors are always cheaper than you, when you come to the selling stage you must build value on your price. Don't expect to get away with closing your presentation without price coming up as an objection!

Most products and services have only a very few inbuilt objections. A very good piece of advice is for you to discuss with the most successful salesperson in your company or business how they handle particular objections.

Inability to handle objections is, of course, a weakness and the true professional must make it a *strength*. There is no point whatever going into the market-place to get business and make sales with *any* weakness. It is quite uncanny how customers always seem to home in on that flaw. You will spend most of your presentation dreading customers' raising '*that* point'.

# ◀ THE THREE-STAGE PROCESS TO ▶ DEFLECT OBJECTIONS

Let's now look at how to handle objections correctly. There are three stages:

- Ask back
- Agree and outweigh
- Provide the answer.

## STAGE ONE — ASK BACK

The first stage in answering an objection is to find out if what is being said is the *real* objection. It is most important that you are absolutely clear about what is being asked of you.

Imagine the objection to be like an apple. Inside the apple is the core and it is the core that is the real objection. So in order to get to the core, you have to take bites out of the apple. Let's take a very straightforward example. Your prospect says that your price is too high. That is an apple objection. You cannot, and you *must* not, attempt to answer it, because there are too many variables for you to be able to cover it accurately or reassure the prospect. When somebody says that the price is too high, it could mean:

- Somebody else is cheaper
- It's more expensive than I thought
- I can't afford it
- I want a discount
- It's outside my budget
- I'm not the decision-maker
- It's my job to reduce the price
- I don't really want it.

'The price is too high' could mean any of these, so the first stage in handling the objections to ask the question back:

- In relation to what?
- How much is too much?
- May I ask you why you say that?
- That's an interesting point, may I ask you why you think it is too high?

By doing this you get yourself back into a discussion, and you may have to keep questioning each statement that is made until you finally get to the core of the objection. Only when you have found the real objection should you proceed to the second stage which is to agree and outweigh.

## STAGE TWO — AGREE AND OUTWEIGH

Now agreement does *not* mean saying, 'Oh yes, I quite agree with that', and losing the sale. That is as bad as it's opposite, making the prospect feel stupid with a talk down statement. The result is identical. So you must agree with the prospect's *thought process*, the reasoning that led him or her towards that core objection. Let me give some examples:

- I can understand your reason for saying that, Mr Prospect, and it has since been proved that ...
- Mr Prospect, I used to think the same but I have since discovered ...
- It's interesting that you should say that Mr Prospect. Some of my best customers used to think that as well but they have found ...

You will gather from these examples that we should agree with the *thoughts* but not the *objection*. We build our prospect. Don't put him or her down. But we outweigh the objection with experiences, results, performance, success, and value.

## *STAGE THREE — PROVIDE THE ANSWER*

The third stage involves answering the objection to your prospect's satisfaction, remembering all the time that they *want* to be convinced. You would want to be convinced if you were sitting in their place.

◀    # *COMMON OBJECTIONS*    ▶

Here is a list of the most common objections that arise. Most professional salespeople have to handle them at some stage in their selling careers. Remember that we are still dealing with *principles*, and that you must fit them into your own particular product or service.

## *PRICE*

I am going to use the price objection as one in which you are more expensive than the competition, and where your prospect's concern is that he or she should not pay more than necessary. The first guideline is to always concentrate the prospect's thoughts on the *difference* rather than the price. Let's say you have quoted £800 and the competitor has quoted £750.

'So Mr Prospect, we are talking about a £50 difference. Now for this small £50 difference, this is what you will be getting ....' At this point re-establish your unique sales points: 'And furthermore, Mr Prospect, by placing your order with me, you will get my support and attention to your business which means ...', and tell him what you will do. 'Mr Prospect, how long do you anticipate this product will last you? Two years, you say. So that broken down is about £25 a year, approximately 50 pence a week, round about 7 pence a day. Now, in all honesty, it makes good common sense for only about 7 pence a day, to have what you know deep down anyhow is a product of real value. And as you have already said, you don't buy the price, you prefer to buy the best possible value. Are you happy with that, Mr Prospect?'

Whenever you handle an objection, always check that you have covered it sufficiently. Look at the price objection in the example I have just given from the prospect's viewpoint, and remember that to win in a competitive market-place, you don't need the best prices or the best products, but *offer* and then *give* outstanding service. So state clearly and specifically what you will do as far as service is concerned. Don't ever fall into the 80 per cent category trap of saying, 'And we give a good service.'

Finally on the subject of price objections, you are less likely to face this objection if you are smartly turned out. Shabby salespeople cause customers to doubt the validity of their claims about their products or services. A smartly dressed seller, on the other hand, builds value on to their product or service.

## I'M JUST NOT CONVINCED

This objection is a core and is very rarely stated as an apple. Let's look at a practical method for handling this customer worry.

'Mr Prospect, I realise from what you have told me that you are not really convinced that my product or service will do the job you want and that which I say it will do. Now if I had the managing director of one or two companies similar to your own here to tell you how our product or service has performed for them, and how happy they are with the results that they are getting, would you then be convinced?' Now if your prospect is sane he is obviously going to say, 'Well, YES of course I would.'

'Well, Mr Prospect, they obviously aren't here, but let me show you what they *have* said.' Now at this stage, bring out your credentials. Every professional salesperson should carry letters of credibility and statements from their best customers. All too often, salespeople waste these; they have them in a presentation file, and they bring them out as part of their presentation when they are often completely wasted. Credibility should be used sparingly, and treated as your most prized weapon.

You can in some instances even arrange for your prospect to speak on the telephone to another of your customers, so long as your referee has agreed to provide such a testimony. Sometimes it may be necessary for you to arrange a company visit for your prospect.

When you have deflected this objection remember, once again, to ask your prospect, 'Are you happy, are you reassured?'

## NO BUDGET

This one is often an apple. 'No budget' could mean

- They have used their budget up
- No budget has been allocated
- They don't really want it.

But let's take the 'no budget' objection at face value — your prospect wants your product but, has in all honesty, used up that year's budget.

So now the professional salesperson must become creative; you must help the prospect to *find* the money. Make it easy for him to proceed into a purchase situation. Suggest to him that there may be other departments that haven't yet used up their budget allocation, and remind him that another department might be very enthusiastic about providing you with the necessary funds because they know that if they do not use all their allocation it will almost certainly be cut back next year. Actively brainstorm the problem with your prospect. Try the advertising department, or the public relations department. What about the research department, or the promotions department? Maybe there is a special fund?

Make sure you know your own company policy. There are times when creative accountancy can make it easy for your prospect to place the order. Suppose you have discovered that the new budget is due to start in March and you are selling in January. It may be acceptable for you to proceed with the sale now but to date your invoice March.

Before leaving the subject of budgets, the professional seller must fully understand the purpose of the budget. They are set as a means of financial control; they are not set for the purpose of building a business. There is not a managing director in this world, whose goal it is to make profits, who will not allow expenditure over and above any pre-set budget on a product or service if it will enable his or her company to make more money or be more efficient. Because your offer is one that the company should not refuse if they are serious about improvement, development or greater profits they should increase the budget. This comes back to your skill in selling the *result* to those who will make that decision. But it will mean that you may have to make a further presentation to the new decision-maker. Read the chapter on closing before you do.

All this, of course, depends on the objection being a core, not an apple.


## I HAVE BEEN DOING BUSINESS WITH FROBISHERS FOR TEN YEARS

This is an objection that normally comes up at the very first meeting, before the salesperson has had a chance to ask any questions and, hopefully, before he or she has made a presentation. It is, of course, quite common and this is what you as the seller want your customers to be saying to *your* competition.

So how does the winner approach this brick wall? Try this.

'Mr Prospect, presumably when you selected Frobishers it was because you wanted to get the best possible value and the best possible service with the right guarantees and the right security. Would I be correct in thinking that?'

Your prospect is unlikely to deny this, and he may even give further details of why Frobishers were selected. At which point the winner will say something along these lines: 'Well, presumably, Mr Prospect, you are *still* concerned that you should be buying the best possible value with the best possible service because that's exactly why I am here. May I tell you about what we have to offer?' And then go into stage 2 of your presentation.

Now, in reality, there will, of course, be occasions when you will not be able to gain the whole of that client's business. There will be occasions when you will most certainly win. But you can always be a winner, and so can your customer, when your prospect tells you what he requires from you, and from another supplier. You can suggest that, for his own security, it's better not to have all his eggs in one basket. There will also be times when you can go for a very small, trial order. Do you recall Chris Bowles's bag of calf food?

At the very least you should come away with a promise from your prospect that he will contact you if ever he should be in difficulties, or need some service or product in an emergency.

## DELIVERY

Let's look at delivery as an objection that you cannot possibly answer. Your customer requires delivery on a specific date and you know that your production schedule makes this impossible. You can only supply two weeks later. You are in an impasse. That objection cannot be answered. The professional seller's approach is to *change the prospect's thinking*. Move him from impasse to your unique selling points. Re-establish them with your buyer and say, 'Mr Buyer, from everything that you have told me, it is obvious that you really do want this product. Now doesn't it make good commercial sense just to wait only fourteen more days to get what you really want rather than something that will just get you by?'

## ANOTHER OPINION

Your prospect wants to discuss the purchase with somebody else – a husband or wife, a partner, co-director, or any Tom, Dick and Harry. As far as home sales are concerned, it's only the real wally salesperson at the bottom end of the 80 per cent category who will waste time making a sales presentation without both husband and wife being there. So I am not even going to bother giving the cure when prevention is so easy.

In the business world, however, the professional seller should say something like this: 'Just supposing they like it, will you go ahead?' Now this is a very important fact to establish, because the objection could have been an apple. If they answer YES, you have pre-closed the sale and it will now be necessary to get yourself in front of whoever the discussion is going to take place with. Don't let your prospect make the presentation on your behalf because he will not do your product or service justice. He can't, as you know a great deal more than he does and only you can answer the various concerns and objections that the other party may raise. So fix a time for the meeting, and explain to your prospect that it is obviously in his interest that you explain your product or service to give it the best possible chance of getting into a GO situation. I sometimes say, 'I'm sure you wouldn't want somebody else selling what you do on your behalf. Likewise, the same applies to me.'

# *I WANT TO SEE THE COMPETITION*

This prospect says, 'YES, I like what you have got. YES, I'm convinced that it's good. But before I make a decision, I want to see what else is on offer.' Or, 'I'm not going to make a decision today, as I have so and so coming in tomorrow.'

The professional salesperson should never fear this objection because you know that what you can offer will be better. It is natural for buyers to want to be sure they are making the right decision. Don't *you* think before you buy something? Don't *you* shop around, look to see what else is available? But there are several ways of handling this objection. In some instances it is quite acceptable for you to talk about what else is available, to advise your client and mention your competitor's unique selling points. These, of course, will naturally be outweighed by the advantages of your own products, but don't make the mistake of not telling the truth. There is a lot of value in advising your prospect of the unique selling points of a competitor, particularly if you know that they are going to be making a presentation to the prospect. If they are coming in after you, you will be stealing their thunder. And while they are labouring their USPs the buyer will be thinking, 'I know this already.' If *you* are going in second, you can demonstrate your industry knowledge and will build your credibility and trustworthiness with the buyer. It shows too that you are not afraid. And if you are not afraid, your buyer will not be afraid.

In those cases when your prospect is stating quite categorically that he will be seeing other companies, always get an appointment to go back in last of all, when he has completed his interviews with your competitors. And get an absolute guarantee from your prospect that he will not make a decision until you come back in again. The conversation can follow these lines: 'Of course, Mr Prospect, I quite understand why you want to see what else is available. If I was in your shoes I would be doing just that, but I really do want to do business with you. Will you allow me to come back again with some proposals, before you make a definite decision? I am sure you will find them acceptable. Let's fix a firm date now.'

Once again let me refer you to the chapter on *Closing*, because there are times when it is not an objection, it is just flannel. In such cases the sale should be closed.

You will no doubt have gathered from all this that the secret is to find the *real* objection, the *hidden* objection. I love this quotation: 'A person generally has two reasons for saying something, one that sounds good, and the real one.'

## I WANT TO THINK ABOUT IT

This is probably the most feared objection of all among speciality or home sales people. There is a lot of gimmicky nonsense talked about coping with this objection. I once heard a sales trainer say that his method for handling a customer who says he or she wants to think about it is to reply, 'Oh yes, and what are you going to use for equipment?'

I find the best and most professional method of all is to say, 'Sure Mr Prospect, I quite understand that. But, presumably, if you want to think about it there must be one or two points that you are a little uncertain about. Would I be right in thinking that?' Most people then say, 'Yes, there are a number of things I have to think about before I can definitely make up my mind.' The professional salesperson will then say something to this effect: 'OK, let's just list those and see exactly what they are.' He or she will then take out a clean sheet of paper and write numbers from one to ten. 'Now, Mr Prospect, what is the first concern that you may have?' Whatever he says, write it down next to number one. Ask the question again, and write the answer next to number two. At most you will have a list of three or four. When the prospect runs out, say, 'Now, is there anything else that we haven't thought of?' If he says, NO, ask, 'Mr Prospect, if I can answer all of these points that you have made to your complete satisfaction, and I am not saying that I definitely can, but *if* I can, can we go ahead?' If he says, YES, your sale is pre-closed and you should reassure the prospect point by point. If he says, NO, the professional seller says, 'Then there must be something else.' Add the new concern to your list and again draw a line underneath that number. As you answer each one of these points tick them off clearly and visibly, before proceeding to the next. And check each one, 'Now, are you happy with that?' Or, 'Have we covered that satisfactorily?' Or, 'Are you now reassured on that point?'

The buyer who says, emphatically, 'Under no circumstances will I give you a decision today as I am going to think it over' will not react well if you try to push a decision. The professional salesperson will say, 'Fine. When will you make that decision by?' When you have got the date, say something like 'Fine, Mr Prospect. I can rely upon that then can I? I will give you a call then.'

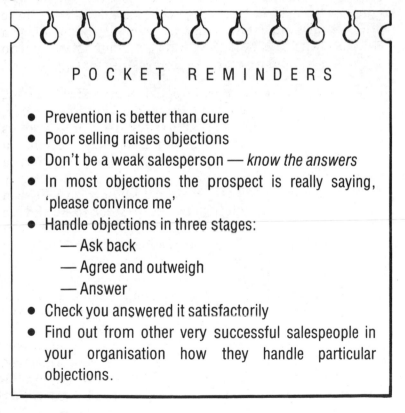

POCKET REMINDERS

- Prevention is better than cure
- Poor selling raises objections
- Don't be a weak salesperson — *know the answers*
- In most objections the prospect is really saying, 'please convince me'
- Handle objections in three stages:
  — Ask back
  — Agree and outweigh
  — Answer
- Check you answered it satisfactorily
- Find out from other very successful salespeople in your organisation how they handle particular objections.

' WISE WORDS '

There is no substitute for hard work. Don't talk about it, do it.

Gerald Ronson

# 13

# *Negotiation*

Professionals must understand that so much of good, modern selling will involve negotiation, because very rarely does a sale depend upon a single item with a single price and a single delivery date. Therefore, in presenting a proposal you will often need to negotiate the parameters to get both parties into a WIN WIN situation.

You must be sure in your own mind of the type of relationship that the prospect is looking to build with you. Will your sale be a one-off sale? Professional sellers should always be looking for repeat business or new opportunities but there are, without question, some occasions when the salesperson will make a one-off sale. Suppose you sell your car or house privately, for instance. You will be very unlikely ever to sell another car or house to the same person. In these cases you will quite naturally be more interested in getting the best possible deal for you regardless of how bad it is for your prospect. You will probably want to drive a hard bargain in this type of sale. I personally don't like that expression, but it sums up an attitude that is often adopted.

If you are attempting to build a long-term relationship, however, it is very important to be aware of maximising the trust and confidence in the relationship while at the same time being careful not to concede to every whim of the prospect. So you need to negotiate.

It is also well worthwhile being aware that if a seller has too much authority to negotiate it can lead to weak selling, to the salesperson giving too much away. In my experience, whenever salespeople are given a lot of flexibility on price the vast majority of transactions are at the lower end of the scale. So if your company restricts your authority and does not give you too much room to negotiate, you will be a better seller and a more proficient negotiator for it.

# ◀ THE PRINCIPLES OF NEGOTIATION ▶

Let's now run through some of the principles of good negotiation.

## THE PERSON WHO AIMS HIGH WILL GET MORE

Salespeople who *think big* get *big results* (but don't catch big caseitis!).

Successful selling, as you know, depends largely on your attitude, so it is crucial that you raise your own level of aspiration but lower your prospect's. If you don't keep your aspirations high your prospects will almost certainly lower them for you. Let me give you some examples of comments that will instantly *lower* your level of aspiration, and thereby reduce your ability to negotiate:

The prospect says:

- We've already had a very good quote

- This is not really a priority for us right now
- You've got to be sharp on the price or else you've got no chance
- We have never bought in large quantities.

The above will *all* lower your aspiration level. Now let's look at some examples that will *raise* your aspirations but reduce the prospect's.

- This is proving to be outstandingly popular
- There is a long waiting list
- These are now selling at a premium
- Our products show hardly any depreciation.

I quite recently had my aspiration level, and therefore my ability to negotiate, totally destroyed. Despite what I have already said about the motor industry, I wished to purchase a new Daimler. I duly contacted our local agent, had a demonstration and then got around to discussing the price and the terms. Naturally enough I was going to see how big a discount I could get for a cash purchase. I was politely informed by the salesman that these cars were now selling at a premium. There was an eight-month waiting list. Jaguar's Daimler sales worldwide had become one of the great success stories of the British motor industry. New cars coming off the production line were selling for up to £3,000 above their list price. And if I *really* wanted a Daimler I would have to pay a deposit of £1,000 and have my name put on the waiting list.

Now one of my personal principles is that I never pay a deposit on anything. But despite letters despatched to all and sundry I was totally unable to negotiate this point. My level of aspiration had been lowered to such an extent that I paid my £1,000 and was indeed *grateful* to have my name put on the waiting list! So all my negotiation skills resulted in parting with £1,000 for some eight months, and a full tank of petrol for my car! So, who am I to teach? Well, there is a lesson for all of us here — *never let your prospect lower your sights.*

## DON'T BE A PRICE CRUMBLER

Many salespeople succumb to the temptation to reduce their prices as soon as they are put under a little pressure. Good negotiators defend their prices logically, by reinstating the value. Your products and services are priced for a very good reason to make profits, and provide security for yourself and everyone else in your company. So don't be willing to concede on price. The art of negotiation is to put together a package that is going to be right for both parties.

## DON'T EVER GIVE AWAY CONCESSIONS

This principle sums up much of what is best about *good* negotiation. Don't give away, but *trade* concessions. Learn to balance what you offer against what you are offered.

*Nothing should be given away free.* Here is a simple example: 'Mr Prospect, if you agree to pay in 14 days, then we can meet your price.' If you are negotiating a price your prospect will often offer to split the difference between your price and his. A skilful negotiator, rather than agreeing to this, will say, 'I just can't afford to do that. But what I can provide ... (offer an extra service that will be of real value to your prospect) if you agree to take the package.'

## NEGOTIATE THE VARIABLES

The skilled negotiator always has something to trade that is *not* the price. If your product or service has been sold correctly, you will have inflamed the prospect's *desire* but he or she will still want to negotiate the best possible deal. Try never to get into a haggling situation over prices. The variables that you should be negotiating should be *cheap* to you but *valuable* to your prospects. So make a list of your own concessions. Here is a list of questions you should ask yourself to help you compile your own list:

- What do we normally make?
- What are they worth?
- What can we receive in exchange?
- What other variables do we have?
- What can we offer that is cheap to us but valuable to him?
- What can he offer that is cheap to him but valuable to us?

## REDUCE THE VALUE OF THE PROSPECT'S CONCESSIONS

This is where the negotiator reduces the buyer's perception of his or her own concessions. Try:

- It's quite normal to do that
- Many companies do that
- That's not going to help us a great deal
- That's not too much good to us.

Such statements gradually erode your opponent's negotiating skills.

## BE MISERLY

This is, perhaps, one of the most important principles of good negotiation, especially if you intend to build a long-term relationship. There is nothing more uncomfortable for both buyer and seller than when the seller agrees too readily on a negotiated package. I am sure you must have experienced this yourself when you have had something to sell. You advertise your house or car or whatever and the buyer makes you an offer which you immediately accept. The buyer goes away thinking, 'I should have made a lower offer because I bet he would have accepted it.' You go away thinking, 'I should have got a better deal. I'm sure he would have paid more if I had stuck it out.' If you are going to trade concessions, you must *trade them reluctantly*. You must put up a fight at every stage, every concession must be wrung out of you. When people reach an agreement too quickly, both parties always feel that they could have got a better deal, and next time they will negotiate a much tougher one. So don't ever say YES too quickly. Don't ever accept the first offer. You must always let your buyers feel that they really have negotiated a good deal. So whenever you are about to say YES, say NO just a few more times.

## BE AWARE OF THE DANGER OF DEADLINES

Your ability to negotiate will always be reduced when a cut off date or a deadline is imminent. The salesperson who is desperate to get one more sale to meet his monthly target is much more likely to concede if he is negotiating on the last day of the month. And if your prospects have clearly indicated a deadline by which they must have concluded the transaction, *their* negotiating skills will also be reduced. This knowledge can be a tremendous weapon, but don't let an impending deadline put *you* in a position of weakness.

## SEE THE BIG PICTURE

Always keep the whole deal in mind. Try and get your prospective buyer's complete shopping list and all his or her requirements. This will strengthen your ability to negotiate because it will help you to trade concessions. Remember to balance the trade-off. What I offer you should be balanced by what you offer me.

## NEGOTIATE THE DEADLOCK

When your negotiations have reached deadlock, there are no more concessions on either side and you have exhausted all offers to trade you will need exceptional negotiating skills. But it is likely that both sides will have invested quite a lot of time by this stage and it may be worth trying to concentrate your prospect's thoughts on the time *he* has spent. Try something along these lines: 'Mr Prospect, we have both invested a great deal of time. We both want to conclude and get this business transacted. Let's just go through it one more time before we admit defeat.'

## IDENTIFY YOUR WEAKNESSES

No salesperson should attempt to negotiate in the knowledge that he or she has got areas of serious weakness. Turn those areas into areas of *strength*, because our weaknesses immediately become apparent. It is the weaknesses that the other side will concentrate on. And the more they concentrate on those weaknesses the more they will undermine your ability to negotiate.

Let's now look at a few situations: The buyer says, 'I like the proposal but this is all I've got.' A weak negotiator will respond by instantly offering a discount. An able negotiator, on the other hand, will put together and then offer an alternative package.

So wherever possible be armed with some alternative packages and remember that if your buyer wants to change the price, you will *change the package*. One price for one proposal and a different price for another.

The buyer says, 'You've got to do better than that.' Be persistent in your defence of your price, rebuild the value of what is being offered and make a promise against performance. The negotiator will say something along these lines: 'Yes, we can do better than that — if you will increase your order to ....' So be ready to trade.

Now, we all know that some buyers think that this tactic makes them good buyers. But you and I know that the customer who uses this as a tactic will, in the end, only be confronted by salespeople who have already inflated the price. I was selling digital watches a few years ago, and I was confronted by small-time buyers who constantly pestered me for larger discounts. Discount was all they were interested in.

So, quite naturally, I inflated the price and gave them their discount. No doubt you have seen slashed across shop windows, 10 per cent *discount*, 20 per cent *discount*. What is important is the figure that is being discounted.

The buyer says, 'I have to get final approval from my board, the managing director, the chairman, etc.' This is sometimes used as a delaying tactic to get a better deal and reduce your aspirations. The skilful negotiator will put a time limit on the decision-making process. Remember that deadlines produce weakness when applied.

The buyer says, 'Take it or leave it.' The negotiator must not get into a confrontation or create a show down. If the buyer says, 'I want a 10 per cent discount. Take it or leave it,' the negotiator must find a face-saving solution. Don't respond by saying, 'That's not negotiable.'

And lastly, for those of you who are buyers as well as sellers, (and we all are) negotiate yourself to get the best possible deal. Imagine you are in a tailor's to buy a new suit. Ask the tailor how much he will charge you for two suits. Let's suppose he quotes you £600. Now point to the suit that you *don't* want and ask him how much that will be. He will almost certainly say £350. You can then say, 'Fine. I'll take the other as that is obviously £250!'

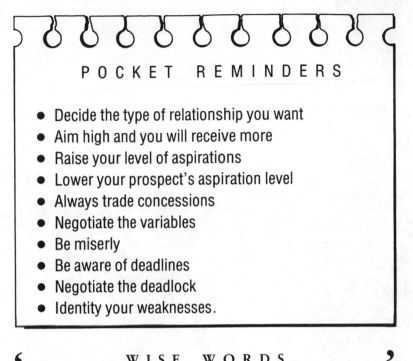

P O C K E T   R E M I N D E R S

- Decide the type of relationship you want
- Aim high and you will receive more
- Raise your level of aspirations
- Lower your prospect's aspiration level
- Always trade concessions
- Negotiate the variables
- Be miserly
- Be aware of deadlines
- Negotiate the deadlock
- Identity your weaknesses.

**'      W I S E    W O R D S      '**

First you must have the appetite to succeed — ambition. When you have no ambition, you are dead. You have to be willing to work.

Sir James Goldsmith

# 14

# *Letter Writing*

A comprehensive guide to letter writing skills is beyond the scope of this book, but I want to give you a few basic guidelines to make written communication for getting business more effective. This chapter contains a few useful ideas that I *know work*.

## ◀ SHORT LETTERS WORK ▶

Research into direct mail has demonstrated that any mailshot must contain a letter, and this letter is most effective when it is a two-page letter written on four sides. Now that is directly contrary to what works in business to business communication. If your letters are *short* and arc on one side of a page, they will get read. If they are much longer they won't, or if they do they will be at the bottom of the pile. Another advantage is that by making your letters short you save thinking, dictation and typing time. That leaves you more time to *sell*.

◀    ## SHORT PARAGRAPHS WORK    ▶

Try to ensure that your paragraphs contain no more than two sentences each. You've got to keep your reader's attention.

◀ ## MAKE YOUR LETTERS EASY TO READ ▶

Have you ever read *Readers Digest*? When you pick it up, what do you read first? I bet it's the quotations and snippets at the end of the chapter. People who read your letters react in just the same way. They want easily digested information in the simplest possible format.

◀    ## AVOID VICTORIANA    ▶

It is unnecessary nowadays to clutter your communications with phrases like, 'Please find herewith enclosed'. Why not say 'Here is', or, 'I have enclosed'? And just as a thought, why do you always start your letter off with the word 'Dear'? If you were talking to the recipient of your letter on the telephone, or face to face, would you address him or her as 'Dear'? You would be more likely to say, 'Hello'. So how about starting a letter off with a 'Hello'? This is, admittedly pretty outrageous, so watch who you send it to!

◀    ## AVOID JARGON    ▶

Let me give you an example taken from *The Executive Training Programme Better Letters* published by the Economics Press in New Jersey, USA. Someone once wrote to a government bureau asking if hydrochloric acid could be used to clean the tubes in a steam boiler. He received this reply:

Uncertainties of reactive processes make the use of hydrochloric acid undesirable where alkalinity is involved.

To which the man wired back:

Thanks for the advice, I'll start using it next week.

Back came this urgent message:

Regrettable decision ... involves uncertainties. Hydrochloric acid *will* produce sublimate invalidating reactions.

Which prompted this in reply:

Thanks again, glad to know it's okay.

This time there came the following urgent, but clear message:

Don't use hydrochloric acid, it will eat hell out of your tubes.

Don't use jargon, whether or not it is specific to your industry, in your sales letters.

◀     *KEEP CONTROL*     ▶

I am sure you have never finished a letter from which you are hoping to gain business with these words: 'If I can be of any further service, please don't hesitate to contact me'. Now I am sure *you* have never done that. But it is really quite amazing how many letters I get with that as a sign off line. The sender has lost control. He or she has given the next move to me, and the future of our relationship is now in my hands.

Some four years ago we purchased a new home. We required some building and decorating work to be carried out. Three different companies sent in their estimates, each having spent some two to three hours assessing the work. They then possibly spent another two or three hours costing out and preparing the estimate. The first one arrived in the post with a covering letter which 'hoped it met with my satisfaction'. It added, 'We value your esteemed business and if we can be of any further service please do not hesitate to contact us'. Guess what I looked for? Of course, you're right, the price! They tried to hide it, but I found it! The second estimate also arrived in the post with much the same verbiage. The third contractor telephoned me and said that he had prepared his estimate and could he bring it round to discuss it with us. He was not the cheapest. He explained why, and what he would do for the extra cost. He convinced me of the value of that increase in price, and he got the work.

There are two builders who have never even bothered to follow up on that estimate! The lesson is: don't write a letter if you don't *have* to, and if you *do* make sure you retain the initiative.

When a tennis player serves the ball it goes into the opponent's court. The quality of his or her next shot is entirely dependent on the way the ball is returned. You as a professional seller must never serve your balls up to the client! Always keep your balls in your court! So the correct way to finish a letter or proposal is with something like this: 'Here is my proposal. I will give you a call within the next 24 hours to discuss it with you. If in the meantime, I can be of further service do please give me a call.'

Whenever possible take your estimates or proposals to your prospects, so that you can take the opportunity to build value. This principle applies to all aspects of professional selling. Always retain the next move yourself. Always tell your client exactly what is going to happen next. Never, in any circumstances, leave your client to make the next move while you sit and wait to see what is going to happen. Many salespeople don't like to follow up or chase a client because it appears they are putting pressure on them. But if, on the other hand, you say that you are going to telephone in three weeks' time or three months' time, you are obliged to do that. Your telephone call will not appear to be pushy: you are simply doing what you said you were going to do. At the end of any visit to a client, always say what you will be doing next. It creates a feeling of security and confidence on both sides.

◀ ## *BE A GOOD NEWS CARRIER* ▶

Try always to include an item of good news in your letters. If you can write something that will cheer your reader you are far more likely to get the response you want.

### P O C K E T    R E M I N D E R S

- Keep your letters short
- Keep your paragraphs short
- Make your letters easy to read
- Don't use Victoriana
- Avoid jargon
- Keep control
- Always include good news.

**'** W I S E    W O R D S **'**

If you want to cheer up, cheer somebody else up.

Richard Denny

# 15

# *Body Language*

The science of body language (non-verbal communication) is still in its embryonic stage. There are approximately 40,000 signals in the English language of which we use about 4,000 habitually. The majority of people can control what they say, not everybody can but the majority can. As far as body language is concerned there are about 700,000 body language signals, 15,000 from the face alone. Obviously one cannot control all those signals, so whenever the spoken word is in conflict with the body language signal, the latter is invariably correct.

The professional salesperson, being a master of communication and a specialist at understanding people, must be able to interpret other people's body language. The professional realises that every person he or she speaks to is different. But there are certain body language movements and signals that we all have in common.

The purpose of this chapter is to make you, the

professional, more aware of people, more aware of what they say and *how* they say it. There are, of course, now many specialist books on this subject but it is my intention here simply to bring it to the attention of professional sellers.

◀           *EYES*           ▶

Let's start with the eyes. It is said that the pupil of the eye will dilate for approval and constrict for disapproval: for things that we like the pupil gets larger, and for things we dislike it gets smaller.

James Burke, on one of his original television programmes, set out to prove this point with two identical girls, twins. He gave one a drug which made her pupils dilate and the other a drug which made them constrict. When the studio audience arrived these girls were presented, and a man was invited to come on stage and choose one of the girls. Although they were identical twins the poor individual replied that they were both beautiful. James Burke said, 'Yes they are, but that's not what I said. Which girl would you choose?' He chose the girl with the big pupils. He then went on to explain that if you show a picture of a naked lady to a male, his pupils will double in size. Now how can one use this piece of seemingly useless information?

If you are in discussion with a prospect who claims that he doesn't really like what you are offering yet his pupils are very large, you know he is trying it on. His body language is saying that he really *does* approve but what he is trying for is probably a heavy discount.

Now, for goodness sake, be realistic! You can hardly go around peering into people's eyes or leaning across their desk to have a better look, but you might just happen to notice!

Remember, though, the pupil size will change according to

the light. When you go from bright sunlight into a darkened room, your pupil size changes. So you must be aware of any light change that may have happened if you suddenly see a pupil expand or contract. This is why body language is so imprecise. There are so many variables.

◄ *SPACE* ►

Introverts generally require more space around them and dislike being crowded. Extroverts, on the other hand, are often more comfortable in a reduced space. There is a zone of space about 18 inches around every human being known as the 'intimate zone'. It is called the intimate zone because the only people who are allowed inside it are those with whom one has an intimate relationship. No doubt you have experienced people invading *your* space. The normal reaction is to back away because it causes pressure on an individual if they haven't developed a close relationship. Space can be used to exert or reduce pressure according to the circumstances.

I understand, although I have not experienced it myself, that effective use is made of body language space during police interrogations. An interrogator will start off by facing his suspect with a space of about six feet and no barrier, such as a table, between the two of them. This provides a feeling of security. As the interrogation progresses, the interrogator will move his chair nearer and nearer to the suspect, until he may even be as close as to have his knees between those of the suspect. At that stage, he is applying immense body language pressure and making it virtually impossible for the suspect to lie without it being immediately obvious.

Now in the world of professional selling you must understand when you may be applying too much pressure on a client or prospect. This will be clearly telegraphed back to you as your prospect's extremities will twitch and make involuntary movements. A foot will start to shake, a leg crossed over another will start to waggle, fingers could also strum which may be telegraphed to you as signs of impatience or frustration.

If you see this type of involuntary signal try to discover what is causing it. Change the subject, talk about something else and let the prospect's body language become relaxed again. If you are exerting so much pressure that it becomes uncomfortable, a natural resistance to you will develop in your client.

◀ *CHAIRS* ▶

Have you noticed that in some offices the visitor's chairs appear to be much lower? When you sit in low chairs you suddenly lose confidence. You are facing your client across the desk, yet looking upwards. It will be very difficult for you to make a strong and enthusiastic presentation in such circumstances. Try and sit on the arm of the chair or, at worst, find an excuse to sit on another chair. If your body language shows lack of confidence you are not giving yourself a chance to close professionally.

Notice, incidentally, the way a person sits down. An introverted person will often move their chair backwards slightly. A more extrovert person will pull their chair up underneath them.

The most effective way of making a presentation is for the buyer and the seller to be on the same side of the table or desk. Face to face encounters, in body language terms, almost imply *conflict*. It's a head on meeting. Whereas being side by side implies that you are working *together*, two people aiming to go forward together in the same direction. Furthermore, if you are right handed try to get the prospect on your right hand side. You will be stronger, more fluent and confident.

# ◀ HEIGHT ▶

Physical height can give an impression of authority and power. We always raise people up for their achievements: sporting winners stand higher on the rostrum than those who come second or third; the most important person in a court is normally in the most elevated position, and so on. So if you happen to be very tall try not to cause a feeling of insecurity by bearing down on a prospect.

One of my great hobbies is horseriding and I often notice the various defence mechanisms and displays of insecurity which manifest themselves when people on foot talk to people who are in the saddle.

# ◀ POSTURE ▶

More is talked about posture in the context of body language than almost any other factor. Be careful not to read too much into a steady posture. What is important about posture is the *change* of posture, not its steady state. You may be in conversation with a customer who is sitting with his or her arms folded. Does it mean that they are bored or uninterested? Not necessarily. It may simply indicate that they are very comfortable in that position. But if a customer who is sitting with arms folded suddenly opens them and leans forward it could well indicate that what you are now saying is of great interest. Be aware, equally, of your own signals in this respect.

# ◀ LIES ▶

There arc a number of signs that betray a person who is not telling the truth. Whenever you ask a leading question, notice the body language response. If you detect an involuntary hand movement towards face, neck, hair or ear lobe, it is likely that what is being said is not strictly true. A further indicator is that the eyes suddenly fix on the ceiling or the floor. Keep an eye on these changes.

◄ *GROUPS* ►

Finally, let's look at the group presentation. The leader or decision-maker within a group of people can normally be identified by observing the group's collective body language. If one person crosses his or her legs and the others follow, the first person to have crossed is likely to be the prime decision-maker. I discovered this by accident.

During a presentation I made to a board of six directors I geared my presentation toward the managing director, whom, naturally, I believed to be the decision-maker. I was selling a very comprehensive training package. I had handled all their questions satisfactorily I believed, yet I could not close the sale and get the decision. Suddenly I noticed that every time the financial director made some involuntary movement the others subconsciously followed. So I fixed my attention on that director and within a few minutes I had closed the sale. I later discovered that the managing director had only a nominal power and that the major shareholder was the financial director.

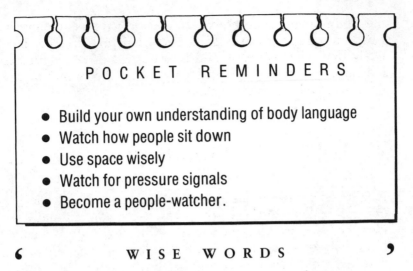

POCKET REMINDERS

- Build your own understanding of body language
- Watch how people sit down
- Use space wisely
- Watch for pressure signals
- Become a people-watcher.

**'** WISE WORDS **'**

**If you do not think about the future, you cannot have one.**

John Galsworthy

# 16

# Avoiding the Negative

The most evil, dangerous and cancerous complaint that humanity inflicts upon itself is to be negative. The salesperson who is unwilling or unable to fully understand what this is and its effect, will never become a champion, a winner and a star professional.

The negatives that do so much harm in the prevention of success, happiness and achievement are all based upon attitudes of mind. It is *what people say* that can do so much *harm* to another individual. These negatives are known as the three 'Cs' — CRITICISING, CONDEMNING, COMPLAINING. Of course constructive criticism is essential for someone's *growth* but so little criticism *is* constructive. It is destructive. It takes very little intelligence to find fault with someone else's work — even a pea-brain would still be able to find fault.

It is what people say that does so much harm. REMEMBER, the negative is always stronger than the positive. Someone might say to you one day, 'You're a really nice person but you will never be a success.' Which will you remember? The negative or the positive? You can receive one hundred compliments but it is the one negative criticism that you will always remember.

The law of conformity states: 'As human beings we naturally conform to our environment, whatever that environment may be.' I discussed this law when we looked at building confidence in Chapter 3. If you are working in an office environment that is positive, enthusiastic and highly motivational, however you may previously have been conditioned, you will start to conform to this excellent working environment. If, on the other hand, the environment is backbiting, full of petty in-company politics, and generally negative, however strong your personality, however strong a positive attitude you may have, you will in time conform and that alone will dramatically reduce your chances of success.

As an exercise in awareness, but also as a bit of fun, let's build a checklist of the characteristics of people. I am going to break this down into the characteristics of 95 per cent of the people and the characteristics of the remaining five per cent.

| 95% | 5% |
| --- | --- |
| They are negative | They are positive |
| They are miserable | They are enthusiastic |
| They worry | They smile |
| They have no goals | They have goals written down |
| They have no plans | They have their plans written down |
| They fear failure | They are self-confident |
| They have false ceilings | They have an expanding mind |
| They have problems | They overcome problems |
| They blame the other person | They look to themselves |
| They cheat themselves | They're honest with their strengths and weaknesses |
| They tear down other people's hopes and dreams | They build other people's hopes and dreams |

I am certain by now you quite naturally conform to the characteristics of the five per cent and you are a winner!

Obviously this is a bit of fun but it is based upon the normal distribution curve — that of LIFE. However, there is a serious side to the checklist. If we base this list on the law of conformity, there is a 19 to 1 chance that we are more likely to mix with and meet people who show the characteristics of the 95 per cent!

YOU as a *professional* must take the greatest care of your ATTITUDE and treat it as the most valuable asset you will ever acquire. NEVER allow anyone to pollute your thinking.

Take the very simple analogy of a barrel full of apples. *It only takes one bad apple to destroy the rest.* In order to prevent this happening, if you see an apple start to change colour, remove it instantly. If you are looking for permanent prevention you could coat each apple with a varnish, thereby protecting each apple from the others. People are very similar. It needs only one person in a group to become negative, and all the others will eventually catch that disease.

So the first stage in handling and then avoiding negative people is learning to recognise the NEG (useful terminology for future use, he or she is a NEG and therefore a PAIN!) They betray themselves by what they say: they criticise; they condemn; they complain; they find fault; they say, 'It won't work', or, 'It's impossible'; they are always expecting the worst; they have no purpose; they have no sense of direction; they blame everyone else because nothing is ever their fault; they have nothing to look forward to; their facial expressions always exhibit a negative outlook; they are bitter with life, people and themselves; they are utterly dissatisfied with everyone and everything; they never lose an opportunity to pull another person down; they are totally unable to give a compliment; they are backbiting and they gossip incessantly; they are jealous of other people's achievements; and they believe the world should treat them better.

The negative salesperson will blame his non-achievement upon the product, but NEVER on himself. The price is too high, the delivery schedule is inadequate, he is given far too much paperwork, he has been allocated a lousy area and, if it weren't for his sales manager, of course he would do better!

There is an expression which says, 'That area is a salesman's graveyard'. If I were to plot on a map every area where this remark has been said, the whole of the United Kingdom would be wiped out as a potential market-place and we would see tombstones lining the roads in memory of fallen salespeople!

It is all an ATTITUDE of MIND.

Negative people continually feed into this valuable asset every little bit of misery they can lay their hands on. They thrive on other people's misfortunes, they search the newspapers for stories of rapes, divorces, accidents and bankruptcies. They are just not aware of the harm they are doing. It is interesting to note that a great deal of research is now going on into the true power of the human brain and thought processes. It is being proven over and over again that positive people are less likely to suffer illness than those who are negative.

The great tragedy about this disease, negativity, is that people are not aware they've got it! People who haven't got it are not aware just how contagious it is or how harmful it can be. It is quite horrifying how many people quite unknowingly allow their greatest asset to become polluted, weakened and in some cases even destroyed by someone else's negative input.

One can make the very simple analogy of a person walking into your home and tipping a dustbin full of foul smelling garbage over your carpet. We all know what the response would be — instant rage and a positive reaction to remove it as quickly as possible. Yet, if we follow that analogy to its logical conclusion, people do not respond in the same way when another is tipping verbal garbage into their mind. They let it happen with no response and you can almost see some people flapping their ears when another is telling them something truly negative.

Most people protect their homes with insect repellents to keep unwanted pests at bay. If during the summer months a wasp should fly into your house there is nearly always an instantaneous reaction — a dash for the aerosol can of wasp death! Yet a wasp sting may only be painful for 24 hours. A negative input, however, rarely lasts for only 24 hours. It can sometimes change a person's direction for weeks, months and even a complete lifetime. So you, the professional salesperson, must truly master your understanding of the negative and make sure you never catch the disease.

I suggest you read this chapter regularly to top up your immunisation. REMEMBER, the negative is always stronger than the positive and your immunisation will wear out in time unless you take positive steps to reinforce your belief and understanding of the horrors of negativity.

Here are seven ideas to work on regularly:

1. Develop and build your own understanding of what is really negative. Do remember that constructive criticism is not negative.

2. Check your conversation with others. Are you being negative?

3. Check your thoughts and thinking process. Remember that if you are thinking negatively the only person you will harm is yourself. So remove these thoughts as you would a bad slide from a projector. Discard them. You have the capacity to do that. Your mind will respond if you are strong enough and willing enough to discard a negative thought.

4. Build a bullet-proof screen around you so that no negatives from other people will penetrate. You can do this by instantly recognising negative criticism or conversation.

5. From time to time, check the company you are keeping. If you have been mixing in the wrong environment, talk to people who are positive. Go out and mix with people you know have positive, constructive ideas. Mix with people who are doing better than you.

6. If another person's negativity does get through to you say to yourself, 'Why did he or she say that?' You must remember that no positive person becomes so unfeeling that they can't see life from another person's point of view. It could happen that someone very close to you says something that can be construed as negative. It may be because they are worried, they are concerned or they have a fear. By asking yourself, 'Why did he or she say that?' You will more than likely be able to understand and, by reassurance, conversation and looking at the worry from a different point of view, turn that negative into a positive process.

7. Have your own NEG repellent. On my live training courses, I train salespeople to always have a NEG repellent as one would have an insect repellent. This is, of course, a fun idea, so please do accept it as such. Whenever anyone says anything really negative to you, just say FANTASTIC — no negative people enjoy hearing that word; they normally run for cover!

'No monument has ever been erected to a critic. Monuments are erected to those who have been criticised.'

**❛ WISE WORDS ❜**

Experience informs us that the first offence of weak minds is to recriminate.

Samuel Taylor Coleridge

# 17

# Don't Quit

There are those in this world who make things happen.

There are those in this world who watch things happen.

And there are those that wonder what happened!

Star professional salespeople throughout the world *make things happen*. They are ambitious and they are goal motivated. They not only recognise opportunities, they also seize them.

For a number of years I was a member of the *If I'da Club*. If I'd only done *that*! If I'd only bought that! I could have bought those shares! I saw that when it first came out! Looking back I think I must have been the founder member of that pathetic organisation. The winners of this world must take risks; calculated risks of course, but they must take them and *persist* until they bear fruit. Winners *make* history for other people to read. Winners *read* history to gain knowledge that can be used to their advantage in the future. But winners do not *live* history. They do not allow their thoughts to dwell on the past or to think what it used to be like in the good old days. The winner must be progressive, moving forward and looking to the future.

Everybody in this great profession has ups and downs. Nobody ever gets to the top in selling without having some periods in his or her life when things are tough. I have never come across any great achiever who has had a rosy path of continuous success. To some extent we are all self-made but it is extraordinary that only successful people will admit it. In mastering the art of *selling to win* you will have rejections, you will have the NOs, you will have days of self-doubt and from time to time you will feel that the grass is greener on the other side of the fence. There *must* be an easier way of earning a living. But *don't quit*.

I don't believe that professionals in any other line of work can ever experience the real euphoria and the wonderful feeling of winning a great SALE. You *will* go through the doldrums, spells when things just don't seem to go your way. But *don't quit*.

There are the good days and there are the bad days. But in time the good days will outnumber the bad days. People often say that you have to pay the price of success. I don't believe anybody pays the price of success or enjoys the *benefits* of success. But *they* pay the price of failure.

But what is failure? A negative word, a frightening word, a word that man fights hardest of all to avoid because of fear of the consequences. Remember: 'The only way to conquer fear is keep doing the thing you fear doing'. Let me absolutely emphatic — *nobody fails at anything until they reach the stage when they finally give up*. You cannot fail until you throw the towel in. You see failure cannot live with persistence, so as long as you persist you will never fail.

History is full of wonderful samples of this great principle.

Thomas Edison, the great inventor of the light bulb, wanted to replace the gas mantle with electric lights. He persisted in his experiments, on his own in an attic. One hundred experiments got him nowhere. His friends told him that the gas mantle had worked for years. What was this silly idea? It wasn't necessary. He became known as Nutty Tom, yet he persisted. After some 500 experiments his neighbours became concerned about him. They thought he had lost his mind. They thought he was becoming a danger to the community and perhaps he ought to be put away. His close friends said 'Tom, you must stop. People are talking about you. They want to have you put away. Don't you see what you are doing. You have done 500 experiments and you have failed 500 times. Now is the time to give up.' He replied, 'No, I haven't failed 500 times. I have just found 500 ways it doesn't work.' Thomas Edison discovered the secret of the electric light bulb during his one thousandth experiment.

Failure cannot live with persistence.

There is a story about a Swede who drove the wrong way up a one-way street in London in a small, open topped car. He realised he was going the wrong way and did a U-turn in the street. A policeman shouted, 'Hey, you can't do that!' The Swede replied, 'I think I can make it.'

Whenever anybody says to you, 'You can't do that. You won't make that sale. You'll never get that deal,' reply, 'I think I can make it.'

Here is another example. All humanity can take some strength from the story of that great jockey, Bob Champion, who discovered he had cancer. Through sheer positive thinking, determination, willpower and belief, he conquered that terrible illness and rode that other great champion, Aldaneti, to win the Grand National.

*You will never fail until you give up.*

# Don't Quit

When things go wrong as they sometimes will
When the road you're trudging seems all up hill
When the funds are low and the debts are high
And you want to smile but you have to sigh
When care is pressing you down a bit
Rest if you must, but don't you quit

Life is queer with its twists and turns
As everyone of us sometimes learns
And many a fellow turns about
When he might have won if he'd stuck it out
Don't give up though the pace seems slow
You may succeed with another blow

Often the goal is nearer than it seems
To a faint and a faltering man
Often the struggle has given up
When he might have captured the victor's cup
And he learned too late when the night came down
How close he was to the golden crown

Success is failure turned inside out
The silver tint of the clouds of doubt
And you never can tell how close you are
It may be near when it seems afar
So stick to the fight when you're hardest hit
It's when things seem worse that you mustn't quit

Anon

GOOD LUCK AND GREAT SELLING